THE HEALTH CARE SURVIVAL CURVE:
COMPETITION AND COOPERATION IN THE MARKETPLACE

THE HEALTH CARE SURVIVAL CURVE: COMPETITION AND COOPERATION IN THE MARKETPLACE

IRWIN MILLER

DOW JONES-IRWIN Homewood, Illinois 60430

© DOW JONES-IRWIN, 1984

ISBN 0-87094-481-9

Library of Congress Catalog Card No. 83–73714

Printed in the United States of America

1 2 3 4 5 6 7 8 9 0 K 1 0 9 8 7 6 5 4

To
Ellen Violet Michael
and
Sophia Hedy Michael Miller

Preface

■ This book offers a voluntary approach to health care innovation and marketplace survival in turbulent times. The approach is based on the cooperative lessons offered by our largest example of competitive health care systems—the 50-year history of the prepaid group practice (PGP) form of health maintenance organizations (HMOs). This book goes one step beyond books like Jeff C. Goldsmith's *Can Hospitals Survive?* which describes a hospital's diversification options.[1] Here we describe the entrepreneurial-political process of how to cooperatively innovate to gain a competitive advantage in the public interest, stressing process roles, skills, and beliefs. We see social entrepreneurship as balancing risk taking with coalition building, marketing with innovating, and competition with cooperation. In sum, we look at health care entrepreneurship in a *political perspective.*

The recent *New York Times* series on the health care field gave the keynote to the 1980s crisis—spiraling health care costs threaten our stagnant national economy.[2] Indeed, at the present rate our nation will have an annual trillion-dollar health care bill by 1994. Faced with such a prospect, both government and business are abruptly and unevenly tightening up on their purchase of health care services. Jeff C. Goldsmith's pathbreaking book analyzes the market opportunities presented by these funding spasms as the inherent competitive nature of the health care field impels the field's rearrangement into a large-scale corporate format of competing health care systems diversifying into HMOs, preferred provider organizations (PPOs), and so on.[3] In such a turbulent world, survival of the individual hospital, physician autonomy, and community governance will be central issues. The challenge now is to move from market analysis to *action agenda.*

The *New York Times* series, after reviewing recent enterprising reform activities, ended on a despairing note—local managerial and political barriers will stifle any swift transformation of the health care field.[4] This sour note, however, is by now a standard complaint: Do not expect swift reform because health care politics is too formidable an obstacle. Our thinking must transcend this tired complaint. Essentially, in the Democratic-dominated years before and after Richard Nixon, it was fashionable to propose regulatory remedies to our health care problems. In these Reaganomical days the "answer" is competition. But this polarity of regulation versus competition is a misguided, stale, and false one. Our health care system, which surely needs to be reformed, was not created in the first place by either of these two social forces. Our system was created by a third force—voluntarism; that is, local involved groups creating local solutions to problems. This kind of local, nongovernmental process is the special political genius of America.

Local health care politics was not always an obstacle, but was once a source of transformation. Did the government or the marketplace create our local not-for-profit hospitals, Blue Cross plans, and so on? Hardly. Therefore, it makes sense to focus on local health care politics and voluntarism as the essential source of reform. Does this mean that competition and regulation are ignored? Certainly not. It just means that neither is sufficient, that both are necessary, and that local communities are best at picking the right mixture of these two tools.

As Peter Drucker has observed:

> It is not "competition" that characterizes American life . . . It is the symbiosis between competition and cooperation organized in and through voluntary, private groups.[5]

This symbiosis permeates our institutions when they are at their best. What is on trial today is whether our leaders can revive this balance of cooperation and competition within and between our institutions. *Health care survival and success hinges on finding and voluntarily guiding this balance of cooperation and competition, on managing the health care survival curve.* Some guiding principles of voluntarism: People need to be able to choose among alternatives in a fair market; people need a voice in governance; and the health system needs and must earn the same peoples' loyalty.

Odin Anderson pointed us in the right voluntaristic direction when he put the survival and service challenge this way: "Can management move from a cottage industry mentality to an entrepreneurial mentality which will preserve the one-on-one relationship of physician to patient—the virtue of the cottage industry—within more complex structures."[6] Within a voluntaristic framework, the entrepreneurial mentality—what we will call *role innovation*—is, following Albert O. Hirschman, two-sided. It balances the risk-taking rebel against the status quo and the political conciliator, who is able to "engineer agreement among all interested parties, such as the inventor of the process, the capitalist, the supplier of parts and services, the distributor, etc."[7]—the enterprising mentality combines competition and cooperation.

Innovating to survive and thrive, then, is the process of making new things happen and succeed by means of the cooperative pursuit of competitive advantage for the common good. This process is basically, as Drucker suggested, a political one. Moreover, as anthropologist F. G. Bailey argues, the politics of innovation are marked by the methods of competitive debate and conciliatory compromise.[8] To this I would add that since health care arrangements are inherently political alliances, the engineering of community enterprises, such as health maintenance organizations, is a process of consensus and coalition building. HMO formation is institution-building.

Essentially, I see the growing disaffection for comprehensive, formal, strategic corporate planning and the call for greater action-oriented concern with institutional culture and consensus as following an analogous development in the city planning discipline nearly 20 years ago. What Richard Bolan then said about urban planning is, I believe, a constructive way to think about health care transformation in today's turbulent environment.

> Though planning has never operated in a vacuum, the scope of today's . . . problems seems to impose special demands for awareness of the complex decision web in which the planner must function. *The community decision arena could be considered the "culture" of planning, since its rules, customs, and actors determine the fate of . . . planning proposals.* Understanding the nature of this cultural envelope will help in determining appropriate strategies and techniques for planning and intervention.[9]

Peters and Waterman, in their book, *In Search of Excellence,* have spelled out the context that envelops a corporate strategy in their 7 Ss framework—strategy, structure, systems, style, staff, skills, and shared values.[10] Within this framework, the approach offered here stresses people who are loyal and innovation minded; possess political skills in debate, negotiation, compromise, and consensus building; are plugged into informal intra- and interorganizational communications networks; are organized in adhocracies; value entrepreneurship and cooperation in the service of communities in turbulent times; and adhere to the humanistic values of voluntary health care.

This book, then, interprets the prepaid group practice—HMO—movement with these voluntary entrepreneurial points in mind. Using Alan Sheldon's conclusions as our premise, I see health care systems building as a local, community, political process calling for new leadership roles, for role innovators.[11] I see HMO creation as a community innovation and decision-making process among leaders of three key groups—payers, providers, and consumers.[12]

The book is intended for hospital and other health care leaders who must make their organizations survive and succeed in the face of mounting threats—HMO invasion and so on—by running their organizations through an accelerated course in marketplace survival by means of selective, coalition action. It is also intended for cost-conscious businessmen and concerned citizens who want more affordable alternative delivery systems (e.g., PPOs). Finally, I hope the book provokes some thought by students of health care policy reform and strategy on the importance of a voluntary entrepreneurial approach—as a political process of community innovation coalition building.

The idea for the book was triggered by a remark in the mid-1970s by a Blue Cross Plan "young Turk" who had recently planned and implemented a prepaid group practice-type HMO. He said, "When we had the opening day ceremonies, top plan management was there, quite enthusiastic. But the curious thing is that they were also a bit nervous and unclear about how the program had been formed. They acted as if it had just appeared one day. The process was somehow invisible." At the time, I was senior manager for alternative delivery systems (ADS) development at the Blue Cross Association (BCA). This remark helped clarify my job at BCA—to make the voluntary innovation process of prepaid group practice entrepreneurship visible, sharable, and manageable. To that end I tapped Blue Cross, Kaiser-Permanente and consumer-sponsored prepaid group practice experience. At BCA we were monitoring scores of prepaid group practice development ventures and consulting with many of these locally based projects. We brought Blue Cross managers, related physicians, consumers, and hospital administrators together to share lessons learned. I then wrote a series of "how-to" monographs on cooperative HMO planning.

This book is organized into three main parts. In the first part, I look at the national health policy framework in terms of turbulence, and offer an action approach to managing for survival in such hard times. My contention is that we can increase our understanding of health care voluntarism, innovation, and reform by studying "role innovators,"—the kinds of people who do the innovating and reform. I examine the evolution of the prepaid group practice movement from Depression days through the HMO developments of the Nixon, Carter, and Reagan administrations. Here we are looking for innovation management lessons applicable to today's turbulent times. In the second part, I turn to the local level of implementing policy—of actual community institution building. Here I look at the prepaid group practice planning process from the perspectives of the three key cooperative role innovators—manager, provider, and consumer. The premise here is that the three key actors can better negotiate and cooperate if each understands what the process looks like from the others' perspectives. I lead off with the insurer-purchaser—the newly awakened health care party. Next, comes the provider, who is central to reform, and third, I examine the process from the point of view of the consumer-community—the base of voluntary reform. Finally, in the third part of the book I look at the issue of the industrialization of health, the limits of this process, and the guidance that voluntarism can bring to this transformation.

I wish to thank the many people who helped in the evolution of this book: the volunteers of the Hyde Park, Chicago HMO Task Force who hired me as their project director and taught me my first lessons in institution building; my bosses at BCA, Michael Henry, Howard Berman, Bernard Tresnowski, and Walter J. McNerney, who gave me the opportunity to gather and document voluntaristic HMO planning lessons learned; John van Steenwyk, Dr. Conrad Rosenberg, Paul Young, and Ronald Nick, all HMO innovators who shared their insights with me; and Governors State University which provided me with the chance to write this book, with special thanks to Ken Whittemore for his support. I especially appreciate the suggestions on improving the manuscript by Odin Anderson, Allan Blackman, and Robert Sigmond. Special thanks to Marion Block, Mildred Lakin, and Wilhelmenia Moore, who struggled to convert my scrawlings into clean, typed copy.

I would also like to acknowledge my debt to several books that helped me to better understand the process of institution building: *Blue Cross Since 1929* by Odin Anderson; *Technology and Change* by Donald Schon; *Dynamic Administration* by Mary Parker Follett; *Why Leaders Can't Lead* by Warren Bennis, and *Managing in Turbulent Times* by Peter Drucker.

Finally, a few first words on voluntary action and HMO planning politics: "If there is a moral to this story," said Dr. Ernest Saward, reflecting on the first 20 years of the Kaiser-Permanente experience in Portland, Oregon, "it is to start out young and poor and not be distracted by apparent failure." In the mid-1970s, the fainthearted, who had a few years before jumped on the prepaid group practice bandwagon, started to jump off at the first signs of apparent failure. This left the undramatic, steady effort to others who were more fully committed to health care action and reform. The lesson is that once the right model, market, manpower and money have been brought together, you still need to have politically savvy community entrepreneurs who can seize the moment, risk dangers, and negotiate agreements to establish new enterprises. This book is for this breed of enterprising voluntarist. As Michael Davis, one of the founders of the health service administration field, said long ago, *"Just a little community leadership can achieve a great deal."*

Irwin Miller
Beverly Shores, Indiana
1984

NOTES

Preface

1. Jeff C. Goldsmith, *Can Hospitals Survive?* (Homewood, Ill.: Dow Jones-Irwin, 1981).

2. William K. Stevens, "High Medical Costs Under Attack: A Drain on the Nation's Economy," *New York Times,* March 28, 1982, p. 1.

3. Goldsmith, *Can Hospitals Survive?* p. 16.

4. Robert Reinhold, "Competition Held Key to Lower Medical Cost," *New York Times,* April 1, 1982, pp. 1 and 12. The last sentence reads, "Few expect any speedy remedies through large-scale private or government programs, however, given the political and technical barriers to sweeping change in such a complex system with many vested interests."

5. Peter Drucker, *Men, Ideas and Politics* (New York: Harper & Row, 1971.) p. 179.

6. Odin W. Anderson, Foreward in Goldsmith, *Can Hospitals Survive?* p. viii.

7. Albert O. Hirschman, *The Strategy of Economic Development* (New Haven: Yale University Press, 1958). p. 17. Quoted in Robert F. Herbert and Albert N. Link, *The Entrepreneur* (New York: Praeger Publishers, 1983) pp. 80–81.

8. F. G. Bailey, ed., *Debate and Compromise: The Politics of Innovation* (Oxford: Basil Blackwell, 1973) p. 32.

9. Richard S. Bolan, "Community Decision Behavior: The Culture of Planning," *AIP Journal,* September 1969, p. 301. (Italics added)

10. Thomas J. Peters and Robert H. Waterman, Jr., *In Search of Excellence* (New York: Harper & Row, 1982) p. 9.

11. Alan Sheldon, *Managing Change and Collaboration in the Health System* (Cambridge, Mass.: Oelgeschlager, Gunn & Hain, 1979), pp. 170–189. Sheldon builds on the seminal article on turbulence: F. E. Emery and E. L. Trist, "The Causal Texture of Organizational Environments," Human Relations 18 (1965), pp 21–32.

12. See Lawrence D. Brown, *Politics and Health Care Organization* (Washington, D.C.: The Brookings Institution, 1983) for a provocative alternative view of HMOs. While Brown sees HMO creation as institution-building, he argues that communities lack adequate local leadership to make this process successful.

Contents

debater, consensus builder. Innovation champion. Debate: Contexting plus pros and cons. Consensus building. The cooperative mind-set: The cooperative outlook and negotiation principles. Collaborative principles for innovating by negotiation and compromise. Prepaid group practice creation as community entrepreneurship: A power-over example. Impetus for an actionable proposal. Who decides? Deciding. Implementation. Evaluation and adjustment. A power-with process: Prepaid group practice creation as role negotiation. Clarification. Integration. Workability. Community health care coalition-building basics: Definition, coalition, activation, and empowerment. The manager and the industrialization of health.

Survival of the fittest—fit for cooperation. Competitive forces compelling hospital realignment: market threats and political opportunities. The hospital's market: The substitution specter. Hospital HMO involvement: Motives, roles, mission, and example. Motives: From exemplary innovation to vertically-integrated systems. Roles: Sponsor, employer, vendor. Debate over mission. Medical center example. Hospital HMO involvement amid shifting competitive pressures. Hospital innovation: Physician culture and symbiotic management. Organizational development and physician culture. Symbiotic management. Symbiotic management's four levels. Hospital innovation decision making as negotiation and conflict resolution. The hospital administrator as innovation champion. Decision-making model. Variations on a theme. Entrepreneurial championing of an IPA: Learning about risk taking by obtaining agreements. An innovation champion emerges to "think consensus." The innovation patron acts to create security for innovators. Exemplary innovation for turbulent times. Impetus. Sorting out alternatives: Internal negotiations and external alliance building. Structuring the decision field to build an innovation enclave. The deciding as debate, caucus, and negotiation. A cooperative outlook: Joint hospital-physician-insurer decision making. Implementation of a prepaid group practice. Physician leadership is key to building organizational culture. The medical director's role in cultivating symbiosis. A participatory approach to medical director recruitment and training. Forming the medical group. The health maintenance issue.

Entrepreneurship and activism: Six points. The challenge of political integration. Debating consumer participation. Consumerism is a hassle. We cannot find real consumers. It gets bogged down. Prepaid group practice: Consumer participation and voluntary action. Leadership as facilitating pragmatic problem solving. Maximum feasible participation: Problems of a power-over process. A Power-over model. A prepaid group practice power-over example. Steps and roles of a power-with process. Process. Roles. The health maintenance issue.

Marketing and innovation: From survival to excellence. HMOs as a growth industry. The industrialization of service. Limits to industrialization. The lessons of Kaiser-

Permanente. Three health responsibilities and three levels of prevention. Garfield's industrial model of health care. Face-to-face relationships cannot be industrialized. A role innovator approach to prevention. Kaiser listens to the customer. Theory V: Principles of voluntarism for survival curve managers. An era of ideals, hard choices, and megatrends. Principles of health care voluntarism for turbulent times.

■1
Managing health care
in turbulent times

TURBULENT TIMES

■ There is a Chinese ideogram that introduces us to survival in turbulent times; namely, the symbol that represents opportunity also stands for danger. Turbulent times, according to Peter Drucker, are characterized by agitated societal spasms that shift us away from stable economic growth, competition patterns, and institutional bureaucracies to decline of traditional products, heightened competition, and major risks to organizational survival.[1] Some of these signs of turbulence can be seen, for example, in a recent article on the Fortune 500 and cost control. It began:

> If there were ever a year for American industry to get serious about curbing the runaway cost of employee medical benefits, 1982 was it. While profits of the Fortune 500 were tumbling and inflation was slowing dramatically, the price index for health care surged another 11.6 percent. Many companies' medical insurance premiums jumped 20 percent or more, and business collectively shelled out $67 billion. . . . [S]ome top managements are at last looking for cures and finding at least partial relief.[2]

In turbulent times, then, growth of hospitals and other health care organizations threatens business' ability to show reasonable profits and government's ability to provide social equity. When this happens, the quality and cost of health care service suddenly becomes suspect in the eyes of the abruptly awakened purchaser—health care's fourth party. When industrial and health care survival become intertwined and perhaps contradictory, the medical-political status quo is agitated beyond repair.

How do we manage for survival in turbulent times? The key to be mastered is competition, but this social force must be rightly understood within a voluntary framework. Chrysler's Lee Iacocca has spelled out the elements

1

of Chrysler's survival course. First, the manager must grasp that competition, cooperation, and regulation are not mutually exclusive, but can and must be deftly balanced. Iacocca asserts that we need to learn from the Japanese.

> We shouldn't get mad at them; we should try to imitate them through coopera- tion between management, labor, and government . . . You're going to have to learn to get together or you get run over . . . So yes, we'll have to have a lot more cooperation without affecting competition.[3]

Second, competitive survival calls for leadership that goes beyond charisma. Managers for turbulent times must be politically persuasive in their organiza- tion's external environment. Third, the manager has to adjust to turbulence and cope with an uncertain future that makes a mockery of formal long- range planning. Fourth, the manager must be resourceful in selecting which products to offer, being no longer able to offer all products to all segments of the market. Fifth, the manager needs to participate in joint ventures— to selectively cooperate—if he wants to manage for survival. Sixth, the man- ager must understand that only some of today's competitors will survive. Seventh, the manager has to get a more sensitive finger on the public pulse and produce services that are not ahead of or behind the market, but *on* the market. He must discern an overall direction toward which to steer his organization to safety and success.

These points provide a take-off platform for a set of health care survival curve management principles. "Survival curve" is a concept based on Michel Crozier's *The Bureaucratic Phenomenon,* which Saltman and Young have productively suggested be applied to health care cost containment efforts.[4] Survival curve is an appropriate metaphor for turbulent times. It replaces the institutional "learning curve" of more stable times. The survival curve is a political power equation balancing basic variables. In turbulent times, institutions must negotiate a balance of forces and factions or die. Basically, survival and success increase as a hospital, for example, selectively enters into cooperative ventures for mutual competitive advantage. In competitive times, cooperation becomes a growth industry.

Jeff Goldsmith's *Can Hospitals Survive?* provides a brilliant structural anal- ysis of the rapidly increasing trend towards competitive forces and marketing strategies in the hospital field. As real competitive threats to organizational survival mount, he sees adaptive hospitals diversifying into three general directions: aftercare, ambulatory care, and alternative delivery systems.[5] Cru- cial to getting this job done is a political process of "realignment" between the hospital and the various health professions.[6]

Everett and Richard Johnson have suggested that hospitals will have to be quite selective in how they diversify since they each, for the most part, will cease to be able to offer all traditional as well as innovative services to their communities.[7] Further, they suggest that the hospital manager in this era of transition will lead by means of persuasion involving trustees and physicians in cooperative approaches to formal planning.[8] Ready and Ranelli carry the Johnsons' ideas beyond formal planning into conceptualizing hospital strategic change as a largely informal, cooperative political process hinging on appreciating and interweaving the perspectives and self-concepts of manager, physician, and trustee.[9] Finally, Walter J. McNerney, former Blue Cross and Blue Shield Association president, has suggested that voluntary-guided survival will take place at the microlevel of the individual hospital in its unique community moving in the direction of health promotion. This will often occur in joint ventures and hopefully in ways that support and do not erode personal and mutual responsibility for health.[10]

THE ACTIVATED PURCHASER: FROM HENRY J. KAISER TO COMMUNITY COALITIONS FOR AFFORDABLE HEALTH CARE

Traditionally, health care's third and fourth parties—the insurers and the purchasers—have been passive members in the established health care alliance. In effect, these parties gave their proxy votes to the fee-for-service providers. Since 1944, however, there has been a mounting call for these parties to become more actively involved in the rearranging of health care finance and delivery into a more innovative, organized, competitive format. Stressing local initiative and community service, this has been a call for a renewed health care voluntarism.

The call began in the closing days of World War II when Henry J. Kaiser urged business to move health care into a voluntary, competitive mold through sponsorship of local prepaid group practices across the country.[11] He was ignored by big business. In 1961, labor leader Jerome Pollack called attention to the overemphasis on hospitalization caused by hospital prepayment programs. Like Kaiser, he saw the voluntary, not-for-profit sector as the potential reorganizer of health care. He addressed the local political challenge of getting diverse interests to work together.

> The interests of consumers and providers of care need to be brought into better balance. . . . We are exerting powerful insurogenic influences on the practice of medicine. This needs to be understood and harnessed powerfully and constructively . . . Composed of many diverse interests, hospitals, patients, employees, employers, welfare funds, insurers, administrators, agents, brokers, insurance commissioners, and many others, the voluntary system needs to be able to integrate the essential social objectives of a system of financing health care out of these diverse interests and parties.[12]

In 1970, the Blue Cross Association (BCA) came out with a policy in line with Pollack's call for local voluntary action bringing prepayment and delivery more closely together. The BCA policy urged member Blue Cross plans to participate in local efforts to form promising alternative delivery systems, such as prepaid group practices. This spurred dozens of plans into local political processes involving diverse interests and parties. In 1976, this message was repeated when William Lilley, acting director of the President's Council on Wage and Price Stability, called for a voluntary approach to health care innovation and reform—one impelled by business and labor leadership.

> What has long distinguished our society from others, as Alexis de Toqueville observed in the 19th century, is that Americans alone pursue their own individual economic goals out of . . . a sense of self-interest rightly understood. In other words, industry and labor appear willing to begin the long and arduous task of reforming the health care delivery system in a way which will ultimately benefit all society because they recognize that such change, in the end, will be in their own self-interest.[13]

Out of economic necessity, the business community is increasingly agreeing with labor by becoming a more active and demanding purchaser of health care services. In 1975, for example, Victor Zink, director of employee benefits and services at General Motors and a long-time prepaid group practice supporter, made an issue of the poor fit between the health care framework as it has evolved and today's health care needs. Construction of the current framework constituted a social good. However, Zink believed that this framework needed to be redone. He asserted that a new framework had to be forged—one where the provider is economically accountable. He said that it is time to:

1. Define quality care.
2. Set standards of utilization and to enforce them.
3. Insist upon cost effective administration in hospitals and to reward it.
4. Ask physicians to exercise restraints in raising their fees and to increase their efficiency.
5. Insist that primary care be handled outside the hospital, that hospital admissions be critically screened, and that hospital stays be shortened.
6. Evaluate whether all services are medically necessary before they are provided.
7. Demand that unneeded beds and hospitals be closed.[14]

GM's motivation was and is clear. The cost of health care coverage for its work force cuts deeply into its corporate profits. In 1975, GM spent $825 million on health care benefits—about $1,800 per worker.[15] This has doubled since then.

Some health care policymakers in the 1970s got the message and urged health professionals to innovate agressively at the local level. They pointed to the hospital–Blue Cross sponsored prepaid group practice venture in Cincinnati as an example of such community-based problem solving.[16] While president of the Blue Cross Association, Walter J. McNerney wrote:

One of the things I fear the most is that we'll apply the current delivery and financing system to our problems, when, in fact, the problems since the 30s and 40s have markedly changed—and we need an entirely new framework.[17]

McNerney contended that such a framework emerges from constant innovation. He noted, however, that many people within and outside the health industry in the 1970s saw the health care field as "defensive, put upon, low in HMO [health maintenance organization] initiative and development, and disposed toward the protection of regulation versus negotiations and options."[18]

McNerney has recently described the potential of local business coalitions to become offensive and contain health care costs by supporting, for example, the creation of alternative delivery systems. By April 1982, he reported that there were over 90 of these local coalitions, the majority of which were sponsored by business.[19] McNerney sees this activity as part of a larger nationwide movement of citizen activism. As people become disaffected with governmental solutions, they channel their energies into local, voluntary coalition building. This activism is not so much confrontational as it is conciliatory and stresses negotiation and compromise as its principle methods.[20] Nonetheless, for coalitions to be substantive and not merely cosmetic, he feels that they must attack "such gut issues as changing the delivery system."[21] This, of course, can lead to conflict. The key is for coalitions to lead by facilitating change but not implementing it.[22] Finally, McNerney points to a project by the Robert Wood Johnson Foundation as promising to provide some clarifying examples of how broadly-based community coalitions can carry out local strategies to build alternative delivery systems.[23]

In 1983, the Robert Wood Johnson Foundation (with the Blue Cross and Shield Association and the American Hospital Association as cosponsors) initiated a project to instigate local voluntary health care reform by means of community coalitions. The project, The Community Programs for Affordable Health Care, aims

> to demonstrate the ability of hospitals, Blue Cross and Blue Shield plans, and commercial insurers to join with business, labor, and others to restrain significantly the growth of health care expenditures while still making high-quality personal health care equitably and widely available. This program is a response to the conviction held by many that these groups need to come together to find solutions to the problems of rising health care costs.[24]

This grew out of the foundation's analysis of our voluntary health care arrangements in light of turbulent conditions, such as weak economic growth, inflation, rising energy costs, high unemployment, lagging productivity, and high interest rates. In this era of limited resources and increased public appetite for health care, the foundation reasoned, community leaders must emerge to rearrange local health care or these and other community service systems will not be economically sustainable.[25]

The program's funding priorities and requirements provide a checklist of essential ingredients for successful local health care reform. Fundable projects must be coalitions that are:

Well led.

Not-for-profit.

Aimed at cost control.

Concerned with equitable access.

Directed by one organization among several involved community organizations and interests.

Cooperative ventures of several committed providers and financers.

Willing to match the foundation's financial risk.

Innovations in community health finance and/or delivery.

Supported by adequate health care purchasing power.[26]

A ROLE-INNOVATOR APPROACH TO SURVIVAL CURVE MANAGEMENT

The management of an organization's survival curve requires leaders who can balance cooperative action in a competitive world in order to build coalitions essential to successful community innovation. There has been a convergence of theories from many fields on the management of such negotiated, cooperative change. Ronald E. Fry has suggested this in terms of health care research, theories in management, organizational behavior, large systems change, and intergroup conflict resolution.[27] Innovation theory, international negotiations, city planning and related parts of anthropology should be added to this list. In this section, a political understanding of the community enterprise and innovation process will be outlined, combining the organizational change ideas of Warren Bennis and Donald Schon with the community change ideas of Richard Bolan, Michael Aiken, and Robert Alford. Anchoring this political perspective will be a discussion of Mary Parker Follett's theory of power.

Role innovation

We live in a profession-dominated world. Warren Bennis argues that the reason leaders often cannot lead is that there is an unconscious conspiracy in the form of the paradigms that professionals hold; that is, their culture of shared values, beliefs, and so on. When these established cultural paradigms do not include the leader's ideas, his ideas go unheeded. He cannot get anyone's full attention or effective cooperation. Bennis suggests that leaders can lead by changing these professional paradigms. They can advance such a paradigm shift by identifying, locating, and rewarding people who are role innovators; that is, people who, in their innovative conduct, are changing their profession's character and practice.[28] Henry Ford, Sigmund Freud, Lord Keynes, Admiral Rickover, and Charles Darwin are examples of role innovators. Odin Anderson's call for a new entrepreneurial mentality in health care is, then, a call for role innovation as a means of transforming the health care field.

Radical innovations, however, almost always meet with organizational resistance. As Schon notes:

> these innovations imply radical changes in all phases of business—new techniques, new channels of distribution, and perhaps even a new concept of the market. . . . Also . . . changes in technology tend to carry with them major changes in social organization, threatening established hierarchies, undermining the security of positions based on old products. Moreover, the more radical the product innovation, the higher, in general, the cost of developing it. In fact, the whole process is marked by increasing risk and takes place in a context where most new product efforts fail.[29]

Overcoming resistance

Radical innovation, then, raises paradigm shift issues, such as corporate identity, market conception, managerial mentality, power structure, and risk taking. In the face of resistance to ideas that provoke these issues, most innovations are filtered out by formal lines of organization, communication, and action.[30] Powerful forces exist to keep the organization "on course." Radical innovations in this paradigmatic context are rejected as "rocking the boat" too much. Given this resistance, innovations must be agressively advocated. Bennis and Schon assert that four things can be done to vigorously promote new ideas: use outside pressure and events;[31] use language to create a perception of the situation as one where survival is at stake and use informal lines of communication to win support;[32] and enlist a cabal of "young Turks" to push for the ideas.[33]

Let me expand a bit on these points. Rickover's use of powerful congressmen to bring outside pressure on his navy bosses to support the development of the nuclear submarine illustrates the tactic of external pressure. Ecologists' use of the "oil shocks" of the 1970s to buttress their arguments for more energy conservation illustrates the use of external events. Information contacts are used to gain access to decision makers. Often, time and resources are at first bootlegged to move the idea along.[34]

Language is also a powerful tool for igniting cooperative action. Schon suggests that metaphor and imagery be used to "create a sense of crisis around events," giving people a sense that the organization's survival is threatened. Usually people see the threat as coming from the outside.[35] Moreover, this imagery should be double-edged—that is, it should reveal both danger and opportunity. Bennis believes that "it's the imagery that creates the under-standing, the compelling moral necessity that the new way is right."[36] Schon stresses that the leader's language has to transcend negative threat and neutral numerical objectives. It must offer a compelling vision communicated by evocative examples such as "become another 3M," "be like our organization's pioneering founders," or "discover another Scotch tape."[37] The essence of a role innovator's impact will often be encapsulated into an exemplary phrase, anecdote, idea, and so on, such as Freud's five cases, Adam Smith's market-place model, "survival of the fittest," or "united we stand, divided we fall."[38]

It is by use of such exemplifying tactics that role innovators persuasively argue for paradigm shifts. As Thomas Kuhn argues concerning revolutionary paradigm shifts in science:

> The man who premises [by giving examples] a paradigm when arguing in its defense can provide a clear exhibit of what scientific practice will be for those who adopt the new view of nature. That exhibit can be immensely persuasive, often compellingly so.[39]

The role innovator is, in Kuhn's view, a persuasive debater who engineers agreement in his profession by a strategy of translating his viewpoint into the terms of the viewpoints of others. This is a political process quite similar to an aspect of governmental decision making observed by Graham T. Allison, who states that "the essence of any responsible official's task is to persuade other players that his version of what needs to be done is what their appraisal [from their own perspective] requires them to do in their own self-interest."[40]

Innovation patrons, champions, and "young Turks"

This process only happens, Schon argues, if someone emerges as the innova-tion's champion; that is, a risk-taking person who will be the organization's entrepreneur for the idea.[41] Combining Schon's and Bennis' thoughts results in a hierarchy of role innovators. First there is what I call the *innovation patron*. This is the chief executive officer who wants to guide his organization by supporting selected exemplary innovations. He legitimates the idea and protects the innovation process as best he can. Next is the *innovation champion* as Schon describes this entrepreneur—a marketing vice president. Third is the "young Turk" or *innovation agent*—a department director, for example, who often does much of the work.

Viewing an organization as a confederation of internal and external coali-tions and adapting Graham Allison's view of decision making, it can be said that looking down on the innovation, the patron supplies credibility if the idea is in the direction in which he wants to lead the organization. Looking sideways, the champion negotiates the coalition-building commitments neces-sary for the translation of the idea into a reality. Looking upward, the middle-manager agent gives "the boss confidence to do what must be done."[42] In practice, this neat hierarchy may get shuffled a bit. For example, the chief executive officer (CEO) or middle manager may play the champion entrepreneurial role of coalition builder and risk taker.

Cooperation as role sets

Since many alternative delivery system innovations are inter-organizational ventures, innovators are boundary spanners. They are often marginal to the organization, Bennis suggests, with strategic contacts in other organizations.[43] Indeed, William Reid has suggested that interorganizational cooperation in health care can "be conceived of as transactions occurring within role sets of boundary personnel;"[44] that is, sets of managers, providers, and consumer role innovators. Bolan has suggested that "the general impact of role relationships is that decision outcomes reflect the values, goals, and interests of those actors who possess the most resources, occupy a favorable position in the decision-making structure, possess the best skills in negotiating decision outcomes, and have the capacity for developing the best tactics and modes of influencing behavior."[45]

Pitfalls

There are, of course, pitfalls to any approach. Role innovator pitfalls include the Pinocchio effect, poor resolution of power conflicts, and polarizing language. For the most part, these have to do with overemphasizing the risk-taking side of entrepreneurship, and not paying enough attention to its consensus-building side. Bennis suggests that the role innovator be ready to deal with the Pinocchio effect; that is, people's distortions of the innovation to include their images and interests.[46] Survival situations lead to power conflicts in a double sense[47]—between different interested parties and between the methods in which the actors are to blend different kinds of power. Poor resolution of power conflicts leads to poorly engineered agreements. This, in turn, leads to poorly designed innovations. Lastly, if leadership is too charismatic, too hard sell, it may polarize the situation and deepen conflict.

Richard Neustadt and Harvey Fineberg, in *The Swine Flu Affair*, identified eight pitfalls in overdoing health policy risk taking. They are

Overconfidence by specialists in theories spun from meager evidence.

Conviction fueled by a conjunction of some preexisting personal agendas.

Premature commitment to deciding more than had to be decided.

Insufficient questioning of scientific logic and of implementation prospects.

Failure to address uncertainties.

Insensitivity to media relations and the long-term credibility of institutions.[48]

Ideological party politics (this was not a swine flu affair issue).[49]

Mistaking a multidimensional problem for a simple one.[50]

In terms of successful implementation, Neustadt and Fineberg suggest that the essential level is the local one where there must be adequate resources, public demand, competent professionals and volunteers, and a committed local person providing leadership.[51]

Enterprise as community innovation and decision making

Michael Aiken and Robert Alford put coalition building at the heart of successful community innovation.[52] Looking at the institution's external environment, Bolan suggests that the innovation developer must coordinate and motivate other actors to participate in the planning of most community enterprises. He suggests that a cooperative approach is unavoidable:

> With relatively few exceptions, the American . . . community has so fragmented and dispersed authority that the proponent of any program or plan is forced into informal arrangements for exercising leadership and influencing decision making. Thus, skill in inducing motivation, in coordinating others' actions, and in building consensus in a contextually appropriate coalition (without recourse to coercion) is demanded of those who wish to see a proposal through to a favorable decision outcome.[53]

Adopting Aiken's, Alford's, and Bolan's synthesis of community research, let me suggest that community health care innovation takes the following form. As the environment's turbulence gets pronounced, powerful organizations traditionally outside the health care field bring pressure for innovation upon the field. This pressure is focused on one or more organizations that have reputations for health care leadership—strategic location, history, capability—essential to build an interorganizational coalition required to create the innovation. Hence, the practical wisdom behind voluntaristic health initiatives, such as the Johnson Foundation project, is matched by the findings of community innovation researchers. Vital for this process, I would add, are role innovators, that is, entrepreneurial leaders. Moreover, as a community decision-making process, health care enterprises go through five developmental stages: structuring and defining ideas as proposals, identifying the properties of alternatives, structuring the decision field, engaging in overt decision making, and implementation and evaluation.[54]

Finally, both Schon and Bennis agree that for the innovation to be successfully implemented, conflict must be resolved. This raises the question of power, leadership, and consensus building.[55]

Power and consensus

Power is the key political concept. Prepaid group practices, health planning agencies, and hospitals are all arrangements that provide power arenas. Participants at a conference on interorganizational research in health care called for more attention to the people, power, and process aspects of health care organizations.[56] In discussing the power concept, James D. Thompson called attention to the poorly understood *cooperative* type of power:

> I believe we in the social sciences—myself included—need to be scolded for our laziness about the conception of power. For decades we have been content to regard power as "the ability to achieve its ends, even at the expense of another." . . . But, I am convinced that this is a half-asked question of power. It asks how power is *divided* or *separated*—and this is an important aspect— but the other half of the question is how power is *created* or *generated* or released.[57]

Mary Parker Follett, one of the world's first management consultants, developed, during the Progressive Era, a comprehensive conception of power—one that acknowledges self-interest, but relates it to a creative agreement-building process. She saw the challenge to democratic society as being "the necessity of combining expert service and an active electorate."[58]

According to Follett, the inherent diversity of human affairs inevitably gives rise to conflict which, since it "is here in the world, as we cannot avoid it, we should, I think, use it."[59] She noted three ways of dealing with conflict: (1) domination, where one side imposes its definition of the situation on all other sides; (2) compromise, where all sides give up part of their definition of the situation so that no side is truly satisfied; and (3) integration, where an imaginative solution is sought and created in which all sides find a place without sacrificing anything essential.[60]

The integration approach is possible when each interest can view a situation in the context of an authority or purpose acceptable to all.[61] Then, different sides of an issue will all share a common situation, though they will all have different views of that situation because of their different interests. This integrative or cooperative approach does not do away with sides, but with their, to use Madison's term, *factious will-to-dominate inclination.*[62] According to Follett,

> We want to do away with the fight attitude, to get rid of sides. Yet there is a sense in which sides are necessary to the richness of that unity. In any conference between management and workers, the representatives of the workers should represent the workers' point of view of what is best for the plant as a whole.[63]

When vying sides acknowledge the authority of the whole (a common situation), act together to take shared responsibility for it, and seek an integrative solution, the sides are exercising cooperative "power-with." Follett contrasts "power-with"—that is, mutual agreement—with "power-over," which characterizes the domination or compromise approach.[64] An integrative leader, then, is concerned with an institution's compelling purpose and situation. He does not use dominating power-over, but motivating power-with. He strives to get participants to transcend their narrow self-interest and definition of the situation and reach for the meaning of the institution as a whole. He leads, directed by what is best in the institution, and by his followers who join him in the pursuit of excellence.

Mary Parker Follett, then, suggested an authority type that makes purpose-guided, collective problem solving itself authoritative. For her, the collective situation is the prime authority. This is what it means to have a devotion to a common purpose, recognizing that many people who do not want to obey the orders of tradition, charisma, or routine do, nonetheless, want to reach agreement on how to cooperatively solve common problems. Follett suggested the rule of "the law of the situation," and proposed that we:

> depersonalize the giving of orders, to unite all concerned in a study of the situation, to discover the law of the situation and obey it . . . Persons have relations with each other, but we find them in and through the whole situation. We cannot have any sound relations with each other as long as we take them out of the setting which gives them their meaning and value.[65]

Thus, different sides of an issue all share a common situation—they all have different views of the same thing. A power-with approach emphasizes that the common situation be carried forward, not, as with power-over, that one interest be maximized. Such a power-with approach does not do away with special interests or their conflicts, but it does harness them in the service of a common purpose.

Follett suggested some basic ground rules for building consensus. The rules flow from seeking a common purpose.

Participants must strive to create a common program.

Mutual understanding and respect must be sought.

Conflict must be faced, but either/or situations avoided.

Coordination must begin at the bottom of the organization and move upward.

There must be effective leadership.[66]

A MOSAIC EXAMPLE OF THE ROLE INNOVATOR

Organizing for survival through joint innovation requires a skilled, dedicated organizer. Such marginal people are part of a long tradition going back to biblical days. Indeed, Moses is the first paradigmatic leader and role innovator. A review of his role serves as an excellent sketch of the role innovator. (What follows may be theologically questionable, but hopefully makes some valid observations about role innovators.)

Moses was a good company man. He was raised by the ruling class of Egypt and thus had acquired useful management, political, and technical skills and knowledge that would be vital to his venture.

Moses gained a sense of survival, service, danger, and opportunity about an alternative to the traditional setup. His mission was to deliver his people from bondage to the promised land. Moses communicated his ideas to people of various groups and professions—for example, he discussed things in power terms with the pharaoh (the CEO) and responded to professionals in their own terms (e.g., his magical feats answering the priests' magic).

He held educational and recruitment meetings to mobilize young Turks. Moreover, in a very brief memo (tablets, actually) he conveyed the essence of the innovation in 10 readily understood principles.

Moses negotiated with the pharaoh using persuasive power-with tactics at first and then shifting to power-over methods as the pharaoh proved intransigent. Essential to this strategy was the use of external pressure against the pharaoh—God demands the alternative. (Moses' own negotiations with God were pretty hectic too.)

Moses had to face risks and was tempted to compromise innovation principles.

Moses had to adapt as the planning development period he led through the desert did not always follow a straight, logical path, but tended to wander as environmental factors shifted.

Moses was a risk taker who needed great courage, determination, and faith. This came from the alternative's promise—his were chosen people. This "chosenness" created a lot of misunderstanding and resentment. Some people took it to mean that the alternative was the ideal approach. This was a power-over, exclusionary interpretation and led to resentment by people of other tribes who did not like such an invidious comparison. There is another interpretation which is not exclusionary but exemplary. This holds that these people were chosen to be an example of the ideal—an example that others could learn from. (Defining health care voluntarism as professional dominance is a power-over, exclusionary approach. Redefining it as the balance of social forces is an inclusive, power-with approach.)

Paul Young, Blue Cross of Cincinnati's HMO developer in the 1970s, best describes how the HMO role innovator works: "Aggravate without overdoing it. Instigate without being too obvious. And influence for cooperation at every turn of the wheel." Prepaid group practices and other innovative ventures are led, as E. Richard Weinerman pointed out, by exemplary mavericks or "marginal people"—managers who champion innovation in a negotiated world, physicians who provide medical leadership in a world of scarce resources, and citizens who seek to create a world of balanced rights and responsibilities. In short, starting prepaid group practices is an inherently political process involving the many diverse interests of the health care arena. Moreover, prepaid group practices, because they philosophically combine the goals of effective organization and health maintenance, offer one glimpse of health care in the so-called postindustrial society.

NOTES

Chapter 1

1. Peter F. Drucker, *Managing In Turbulent Times* (London: Pan Books, 1981), pp. 8–10.

2. Louis S. Richman, "Health Benefits Come Under The Knife," *Fortune,* May 2, 1983, p. 95.

3. Charles E. Dole, "Mr. Auto Surveys Chrysler's Survival Course," *Christian Science Monitor,* April 21, 1983, p. 14.

4. Richard B. Saltman and David W. Young, "The Hospital Power Equilibrium," *Journal of Health Politics, Policy and Law* 6, no. 3 (Fall 1981), p. 401.

5. Jeff Goldsmith, *Can Hospitals Survive?* (Homewood, Ill.: Dow Jones-Irwin, 1981), p. 16.

6. Ibid., p. 105.

7. Everett A. Johnson and Richard L. Johnson, *Hospitals in Transition* (Rockville, Md.: Aspen Systems Corp., 1982), p. 5.

8. Ibid., p. 78.

9. R. K. Ready and F. E. Ranelli, "Strategic and Nonstrategic Planning in Hospitals," *Health Care Management Review,* Fall 1982, pp. 36–38.

10. Walter J. McNerney, "Control of Health Care Costs in the 1980s," *The New England Journal of Medicine* 303, no. 19 (November 6, 1980), pp. 1091–92 and 1094.

11. Paul DeKruif, *Kaiser Wakes the Doctors* (New York: Harcourt Brace Jovanovich, 1943), pp. 10–13.

12. Jerome Pollack, "The Union Health Movement as Voluntarism," in *Voluntary Action and the State,* ed. Iago Goldston, M.D. (New York: International Universities Press, 1961), pp. 115–16.

13. William Lilley, Preface, *The Complex Puzzle of Rising Health Care Costs* (Washington, D.C.: Council on Wage and Price Stability, December 1976), pp. ii–iii.

14. Victor Zink, "As Others See Us," *Hospitals,* March 6, 1976, p. 68.

15. Richard Terrill, "General Motors Will Sing Out, Loud and Clear," *Perspective,* Summer 1976, p. 2.

16. Elizabeth M. Meyer, "Renewed Voluntary Spirit Needed, Says Blue Cross," *Modern Health Care,* April 1977, p. 56.

17. Walter J. McNerney, "Five Major Health Field Issues," *Hospital Financial Management* 30 (September 1976), p. 50.

18. Walter J. McNerney, "The Role of the Executive," *Hospital and Health Services Administration,* Fall 1976, p. 13.

19. Walter J. McNerney, "Health Care Coalitions," paper presented at the 1982 Michael M. Davis Lecture, Center for Health Administration Studies, Chicago, May 1982, p. 1.

20. Ibid., pp. 4–5.

21. Ibid., p. 10.

22. Ibid., p. 20.

23. Ibid., p. 15–16.

24. Untitled Brochure, *Community Programs for Affordable Health Care (Chicago: American Hospital Association, March, 1982), p. 1.*

25. Ibid., pp. 1–2.

26. Ibid., pp. 3–5.

27. Ronald E. Fry, book review of *Managing Change and Collaboration in the Health System,* in *New England Journal of Medicine* 303, no. 19, p. 1131.

28. Warren Bennis, *The Unconscious Conspiracy* (New York: AMACOM, 1976), pp. 91–92.

29. Donald A. Schon, "Champions for Radical Innovation," *Harvard Business Review,* Fall 1973, p. 83.

30. Donald A. Schon, *Technology and Change* (New York: Delacorte Press, 1967), p. 117.

31. Bennis, *Conspiracy,* p. 90; Schon, *Technology,* p. 116.

32. Bennis, *Conspiracy,* p. 93; Schon, *Technology,* p. 127.

33. Bennis, *Conspiracy,* p. 39.

34. Schon, *Technology,* p. 116.

35. Ibid., p. 127.

36. Bennis, *Conspiracy,* p. 83.

37. Schon, *Technology,* pp. 131–133.

38. Bennis, *Conspiracy,* p. 93.

39. Thomas Kuhn, *The Structure of Scientific Revolutions,* 2d ed. (Chicago: University of Chicago Press, 1970), p. 94.

40. Graham T. Allison, *Essence of Decision* (Boston: Little, Brown, 1971), p. 177.

41. Schon, *Technology,* p. 117.

42. Allison, *Essence,* p. 176.

43. Bennis, *Conspiracy,* p. 94.

44. William Reid, "Interorganizational Cooperation: A Review and Critique of Current Theory," in *Proceedings of Inter-Organizational Research in Health Conference,* ed. Paul E. White, HEW document PB 198 807 (Springfield, Va.: National Technical Information Service, 1970), p. 89.

45. Richard S. Bolan, "Community Decision Behavior: The Culture of Planning," *AIP Journal,* September 1969, pp. 301 and 304.

46. Bennis, *Conspiracy,* p. 93.

47. Bennis, *Conspiracy,* p. 86; Schon, *Technology,* pp. 127–29.

48. Richard E. Neustadt and Harvey V. Fineberg, M.D., *The Swine Flu Affair,* (Atlanta, Ga.: Center for Disease Control, HEW, 1978), pp. 1–2.

49. Ibid., p. 2.

50. Ibid., p. 99.

51. Ibid., p. 69.

52. Michael Aiken and Robert R. Alford, "Community Structure and Innovation," *American Sociological Review,* August 1970, pp. 662–63.

53. Bolan, "Community Decision," p. 309.

54. Ibid., pp. 302–03.

55. Bennis, *Conspiracy,* pp. 86–88; Schon, *Technology,* pp. 133–38.

56. Paul E. White, ed., *Proceedings of Inter-Organizational Research In Health: Conference,* p. 150.

57. James D. Thompson, "Thoughts on Inter-Organizational Relations," in ibid., pp. 159–60.

58. Mary Parker Follett, *The New State* (New York: Peter Smith, 1965), p. 175.

59. Henry C. Metcalf and L. Urwich, eds., *Dynamic Administration: Collected Papers of Mary Parker Follett* (New York: Harper & Row, 1940), pp. 30–31.

60. Ibid., pp. 32–33.

61. Ibid., pp. 59–60.

62. The opposite of mutuality or cooperation is faction which James Madison defined as follows: "By faction, I understand a number of citizens, whether amounting to a majority or minority of the whole, who are united and actuated by some common impulse of passion, or of interest, adverse to the rights of other citizens, or to the permanent and aggregate interests of the community." See Henry S. Commager, ed., *Selections from the Federalists,* (New York: Appleton-Century-Crofts, 1949), p. 11.

63. Metcalf, *Dynamic,* p. 73.

64. Ibid., p. 101.

65. Ibid., pp. 32–33.

66. Ibid., p. 30.

◾2

Prepaid group practice evolution's lessons for today's survival curve manager

PREPAID GROUP PRACTICE AS AN INNOVATION

◾ Our best example of competitive alternative delivery systems is the prepaid group practice movement. Although a variety of prepaid group practice plans have prospered over the years, they have never achieved the universal availability of the dominant fee-for-service, solo practice, traditionally insured health care system. Nonetheless, in the past 15 years, prepaid group practice has gained considerable attention as a proven alternative delivery system. Prepaid group practice has been broadly defined as a

> medical care delivery system which accepts responsibility for the organization, financing, and delivery of health services for a defined population. Essentially, it combines a financing mechanism—prepayment—with a particular mode of delivery—group practice—by means of a managerial–administrative organization responsible for ensuring the availability of health services for a subscriber population.[1]

In a prepaid group practice program, consumers prepay premiums to a plan which takes those funds and invests in appropriate health care resources and arrangements which the plan projects its members will need in the coming year. It is, therefore, unlike an insurance company which covers the financial risk of expense if, while sick, you find the appropriate health care resource. Rather, it is more like a private school or a fire department in that it *assures* you service as you need it. Prepaid group practice programs, therefore, are called *direct service programs* because they assure access to care.

Despite some key differences, the origin of prepaid group practice is similar to that of the Blue Cross prepayment concept. Both types of health care plans were conceived during the Depression. Both were sponsored locally, founded on the value of self-help, applied the prepayment concept to health

17

care, and were initially rejected by organized medicine as being socialistic. The Blue Cross organization prospered and became a mid-20th century success story. Prepaid group practice grew more slowly. The difference in the rate of development of these two health care movements can be explained in part by the difference in the kinds of innovations they were and the needs of the day. The Blue Cross concept was a *complementary innovation;* that is, it helped sustain existing medical care arrangements. As a third party, it merely rationalized the flow of money from first to second party—from consumer to hospital. Prepayment insured consumers against large hospital bills, and it assured economically endangered hospitals that they would have a steadier inflow of funds. Thus, the Blue Cross concept reinforced and conserved the traditional fee-for-service, solo practice, nonprofit community hospital arrangement that had been dominant since the turn of the century. Once organized medicine realized that Blue Cross was a complementary innovation, it no longer opposed the concept.[2]

Prepaid group practice plans were *alternative innovations;* that is, they intended to compete with, though not replace, the dominant medical care system. Besides being prepayment plans, they followed the then atypical professional pattern established by the Mayo Clinic—salaried physicians practicing as a group. These prepaid group plans combined second- and third-party roles. They assumed responsibility for bringing people, payers, and providers together. In marketing terms, prepaid group practice plans rebundled medical and hospital services in a prepayment plan. Politically, they realigned *some* consumers, payers, and providers in a community into organized alliances. Although not as radical an innovation as some national health service schemes that would replace the dominant fee-for-service alignment, the prepaid group practice concept was branded as a radical, socialistic innovation.

More recently, in the 1970s, the Carter administration boosted HMO development seeing in it a TVA-like *"yardstick innovation"*—a government-involved segment of an industry that can be used to measure the performance of other industry segments. As Paul Starr has suggested, "The primary function of HMOs in the long run, in addition to the services they provide their members, may turn out to be as a yardstick for social policy, indicating what kinds of advantages are possible from more systematic organization of medical care."[3] Beyond this yardstick function is prepaid group practice as an *exemplary innovation;* that is, as showing the nongovernmental sectors *how* to create alternative delivery systems (ADSs) both to survive and to thrive. *Exemplary innovations change organizational and social cultures.*

PREPAID GROUP PRACTICE AS A SOCIOPOLITICAL SYSTEM

Prepaid group practices (PGPs) are organized and financed to provide comprehensive health care services and not just in-hospital benefits usually emphasized by the traditional system. Prepaid plans monitor the use of expensive hospital service in order to substitute an appropriate, less costly ambulatory service whenever possible. Prepaid group practices are effective in reducing hospital utilization. In 1971, a report was issued involving 8 million federal employees enrolled in the Federal Employee Health Program during 1961–68. This report revealed that the aggregate number of inpatient hospital days per 1,000 employees per year in prepaid group practice plans was roughly one half that of those enrolled in traditional health plans, such as Blue Cross Plans and commercial insurers.[4]

How prepaid group practices achieve this result cannot be identified precisely. Some enthusiasts credit one or another operating principle exclusively rather than the interaction of all the operating principles. For example, some believe that the "reversal of economics"—that is, giving financial incentives to providers for maintaining people's health—alone can compel physicians to change their hospital usage practices. It is more likely that this economic incentive works only when linked by doctors and managers with the other operating principles or ideals.

Fundamentally, prepaid group practices are not industrial systems, but social and cultural systems where ideals and beliefs are key factors. Odin Anderson has suggested that in all modern societies, various health care equilibriums are reached in terms of how often people go to particular health care facilities to be treated by particular professionals. He observed that the "current equilibrium levels involve overuse, overbedding, overdoctoring, and excessive costs . . . and that these shared problems are being questioned everywhere."[5] What makes prepaid group practice unique is that it provides our country with an alternative equilibrium and alliance—one that acts against excessive hospitalization.

These alternative delivery systems have demonstrated that a "hospital-without-walls" equilibrium—one that assumes responsibility for the organized provision of health care of a defined population—can be professionally and socially acceptable. E. Richard Weinerman, M.D. called attention to this cultural dimension of prepaid group practice acceptance in terms of "marginal man." According to sociologists, the marginal man is one who innovates and straddles two separate cultures, belonging solidly to neither old nor new worlds. In this sense, patient, doctor, and manager in the prepaid group plan are marginal—that is, working to reform the traditional equilibrium into alternative delivery systems.[6]

What is now changing, however, is the social setting of this alternative health care alliance. Large purchasers of health care services—corporations like General Motors, the United Auto Workers, and the federal government to name a few—are demanding organized and accountable systems of care that emphasize comprehensive services. So, marginal prepaid group practice people now have the winds of change and acceptance at their backs. A realignment of health care allies is well underway. Transformation is no longer marginal but central to American health care.

ROLE INNOVATION ACTION LESSONS FROM THE EARLY YEARS

This prepaid group practice alternative mutuality of interest or alliance had its proponents in the health care crisis of the Depression years. The prestigious Committee on the Cost of Medical Care advocated the emerging prepaid group practice concept in its 1932 recommendations.

> The committee recommends that organized groups of consumers unite in paying into common fund agreed annual sums in weekly or monthly installments, and in arranging with organized groups of medical practitioners working in private group clinics, hospital and medical staffs or community medical centers, to furnish them and their families with virtually complete medical services. By "organized groups of consumers" the committee means industrial, fraternal, educational, or other reasonably cohesive groups.[7]

By the Depression, the medical profession had established the fee-for-service, solo-practitioner medical care alignment. Organized medicine resisted almost all alternatives. As medical historian Dr. George Rosen observes: "Since the turn of the century a marked characteristic of the organized medical profession in the United States has been a generally negative attitude to innovation in the organization, financing, and delivery of health care."[8] Originating in the last decade of the 19th century, this resistance was economic and social. It was economic in that many solo-practitioner physicians then were economically threatened—often by competition from more institutionally related practitioners doing, for example, contract or lodge medicine. These alternative forms had been experimented with more and more in the last half of the 19th century, and fee-for-service, solo-practitioner hostility grew as their economic situation suffered severely from the competition. Physicians organized from 1890 to 1940 to control the practice of medicine and save the traditional form of practice.[9] For a long period, professional autonomy—which gave organized medicine control over the health care market—and the public good were seen as congruent. As previously noted, this perception of mutuality has recently become attenuated and alternative innovations are again being sought—alternatives that stress economic accountability to the purchasers of services.

Prepaid group practice programs, despite organized medicine's resistance, were organized around the country almost always by *local physicians.* The consumer prepaid group practice movement was led by a modern Moses. His story is one of marginality and mission. Raised in Lebanon, Dr. Michael Shadid obtained his medical training in the United States and practiced in the same rural county in Oklahoma for 17 years. As a successful, middle-aged physician, he took stock of his life in 1928 and decided to use his skills to act on his democratic ideals, thereby risking his privileges.[10] Dr. Shadid started a hospital-based prepaid group practice in rural Elk City, Oklahoma, in 1929. His purpose was to organize with consumers a health care system in the tradition of the Mayo Clinic model. His mission was to increase the availability of quality medicine then exemplified by the Mayo Clinic, and to do so democratically in cooperation with organized consumers. The local grange's patronage was a vital element in his program's viability. Over the years, Dr. Shadid became a leading champion of consumer-sponsored prepaid group practice plans. He traveled widely preaching the message that consumers could organize themselves into cooperative associations and build such alternatives.[11] He offered four commandments or principles: group practice, prepayment, preventive medicine, and consumer participation.[12]

In 1933, a few years after the Elk City operation got underway, an analogous, but corporate-style venture was started in California. Several elements of the program parallel those of Elk City. Again a physician in the hinterlands was the innovator, the model was group practice linked to prepayment, and the goal was to provide high-quality, group care to the underserved. This time, however, the socioeconomic setting was industrial. In the Depression years, a young physician was having trouble building a practice in Los Angeles. Thinking entrepreneurially, this "Henry Ford of health care" headed for the desert where there were patients and no competing physicians. Dr. Sidney Garfield arranged to provide both industrial accident and personal medical care to 5,000 workers who were building the aquaduct from the Colorado River to Los Angeles. Risking his own personal belongings, he built and equipped a small hospital and purchased an ambulance.[13] This venture added to the experience of the Elk City program the elements of dealing with employers and their insurance carriers.

> Garfield charged the insurance carriers $1.50 per man per month and the worker an equal sum, a nickel a day, and in return provided comprehensive care. Workers, contractors, the doctors, and the insurance companies were happy with this plan, operated without charity or hardship on anyone. The key advantage of the scheme lay in predictability—in steady income for the medical group and in a ready source of care at low cost for the workers.[14]

The predictable steady income allowed Garfield to budget for the recruiting of a medical group and the construction of a mini-hospital in the Mojave Desert adequate to meet the needs of the workers. Ironically, fierce economic competition amongst fee-for-service physicians in the city had forced Dr. Garfield out into the hinterlands where the absence of organized medicine opposition permitted an alternative approach. Thus, the Depression years demanded, in some places, innovative arrangements when the medical care status quo proved ineffective in providing access to care.

In 1938, Henry J. Kaiser recruited Dr. Garfield to establish a hospital-based prepaid group practice program for his workers (and later their families) at the Grand Coulee Dam project in rural Washington. Later, as World War II came and Kaiser Industries expanded up and down the West Coast, so did the Kaiser prepaid health program. This included moving into urban areas such as Richmond, California, and Portland, Oregon, where existing medical resources were inadequate to meet the needs of the sudden growth in population on the West Coast during the war years.[15]

It is important not to overlook the role of young Turks in the creation of the Kaiser–Permanente system. Dr. Raymond M. Kay, founder and former medical director of the Southern California Permanente Medical Group, points out that Dr. Garfield was one of a group of young medical mavericks trained at the Los Angeles County General Hospital who were dissatisfied with traditional fee-for-service, solo-practice medicine. These physicians were aware of both the economic burden on consumers of high-quality medical care and the poor utilization and development of medical skills in conventional practice. This discontent led to this cadre of young Turks to be on the lookout for an opportunity to organize in some alternative way. This is what the Henry J. Kaiser–Dr. Garfield connection appeared to them to be. They enlisted in Garfield's enterprise during the war with the intention of going public thereafter. Moreover, some of them, such as Dr. Kay, made substantial creative contributions to the development of the innovative Kaiser–Permanente program. In short, these young Turks were active followers who motivated their leader. He, in turn, led by harnessing their drive and ideas.[16] Over the years, it was Henry J. Kaiser who asked the entrepreneurial question, "Why aren't we doing this all over the country?"[17]

These two stories illustrate many prepaid group practice innovation lessons vital to today's survival curve manager:

The venture is led by a champion—or maverick—who is a physician.

The champion allies himself with a patron who can provide protection, money, and a market; that is, an organized consumer-employee group.

The champion is motivated by an active fellowship of young Turks.

There must be real demand by the population for access to medical care.

The champion brings together money, manpower, and market at the right moment.

The champion rides with historical events.

The champion is a risk taker with a mission.

The medical champion thinks in entrepreneurial terms—Shadid and Garfield were physician role innovators.

CONTINUED GROWTH AND VARIATION ON THE BASIC PGP THEME

Over the years, various types of prepaid group practice programs were established.[18]

The Los Angeles-based Ross–Loos Medical Group was established in 1929. This program was physician initiated and run. (The plan has recently been sold by its physician owners.) The Group Health Association (GHA) was founded in 1937 by federal workers in Washington, D.C. GHA is a consumer cooperative. It is health center based. Hospitalization is available through contracts with Blue Cross and with community hospitals where GHA physicians have staff privileges. New York City-based Health Insurance Plan (HIP) was created as a prepayment plan which contracted with a network of independent medical groups. Hospitalization is covered *not* by HIP but by a separate, complementary Blue Cross Plan policy, though HIP is now developing its own hospital capacity. The Group Health Cooperative of Puget Sound (GHC) was started by consumers after World War II. Hospital based, it has a system of ambulatory satellite clinics. Unlike the Kaiser program (also centralized and hospital based), GHC has a consumer board, and the hospital and medical staff are under one corporation rather than two. Over the years, unions, universities, insurers, and hospitals have also sponsored prepaid group programs. Blue Cross Plans are, for example, heavily involved in network model HMOs that include hospital coverage.

In the following years, two mutually reinforcing events fueled the growth of the traditional medical economy: the Hill-Burton Act was passed which provided funds for hospital construction (but not for group practice facilities), and collective bargaining for traditional health care benefits became legal. Unions sought and obtained Blue Cross and Blue Shield coverage for their members. Thus, negotiated benefit dollars flowed into the rapidly expanding world of hospitals, and the nation funded a hospital-based health care system. Again, professional autonomy won out, and restructuring the health care system was not seen as an economic necessity.

Nonetheless, prepaid group practice programs continued to be formed and to expand. The growth of the Kaiser program produced the next point of interest in alternative delivery system evolution. In 1954, organized medicine in California's San Joaquin Valley, pressured by the competitive possibility of the coming of the Kaiser system, formed an innovative program of their own—a medical care foundation. The medical care foundation approach was quite an imaginative example of the Pinocchio effect. It imitated the organization of prepaid group practice while retaining the traditional fee-for-service, solo-practice pattern. The San Joaquin Foundation for Medical Care worked in partnership with traditional health insurance carriers who marketed policies, set the premium rates, and underwrote the risk involved. Later, the

San Joaquin Foundation spun off a prepayment plan—the San Joaquin Health Care Plan—which is at *economic risk* for providing comprehensive health care services to its members. It contracts with the foundation to provide these services. This program is an example of an individual practice association (IPA).

GENETIC, BUT NOT IMMUTABLE, CODE: THE PRINCIPLES OF PREPAID GROUP PRACTICE

Since its inception, the Kaiser prepaid group practice has been guided by the following principles—its "genetic code." These principles define an excellent organization which matches an integrated structure with complementary professional practice and management norms, economic incentives, and the value of freedom of choice:

1. Group medical practice.
2. Integrated facilities. Combining inpatient and outpatient facilities.
3. Prepayment. The prepayment comes as directly as possible to the providers of care.
4. Reversal of economics. Both the hospitals and the doctors are better off if the patient remains well.
5. Voluntary enrollment. Insisting that at least one alternative means of health insurance be offered (i.e., dual choice) to each individual within the group.
6. Physician responsibility. The physician's acceptance of responsibility for providing comprehensive care to the membership, and his responsible role as a partner in administering the program.[19]

Group Health Cooperative of Puget Sound adds a principle that extends responsibility to include the consumer:

7. Responsibility for the planning and operation of the health delivery system is defined and shared among consumers and providers.[20]

To these we can add an eighth principle:

8. Self-capitalization. This means that the program has a fiscal policy of being economically self-sustaining with less than 1 percent of its capital coming from philanthropic or government sources.[21] This principle is shared by the nation's largest consumer-governed PGP—Group Health Cooperative of Puget Sound. Group Health from the outset has been committed to expansion founded by the sale of bonds to its membership.[22]

Although "the genetic code" sounds like an immutable set of commandments, in practice the Kaiser program applies these principles in a flexible way[23] adapting them to what John Boardman, who was one of their best entrepreneur developers, called *local medical geopolitics*. In Hawaii, each clinic has only one doctor. In Denver, the facilities are not integrated; that is, the hospital is not owned. In Cleveland, there is a strong community advisory board. Moreover, Kaiser–Permanente has learned over the years some basic cultural points about starting prepaid group practice plans. Anticipating Peter and Waterman's seven Ss, the Kaiser people stress corporate commitment, skilled professionals, sharing of a common philosophy, and so on.

Having reviewed the evolution of prepaid group practice plans and their basic operating principles, it is an appropriate time to discuss some elements of health care systems and to compare these elements under alternative and traditional health care systems.

COMPARISON OF HEALTH CARE SYSTEMS

The prepaid group practice plan is an alternative to the more prevalent fee-for-service, solo practice of medicine and the traditional insurance reimbursement system. Medical care foundations and IPAs represent a partial conversion of the traditional system to the prepaid group practice plan format. Like prepaid group practice, foundations are organized, direct-service, prepayment plans that assure access to service in exchange for prepaid per capita payments, but they maintain key characteristics of the traditional system solo practice and fee-for-service physician reimbursement. (Prepaid group practice networks like the Health Insurance Plan (HIP) of New York, because of their medical group format, are more centralized than foundations. However, since these groups are independent of the prepayment plan they are, like medical care foundations, less centralized than pure hospital-based Kaiser programs.)

Table 1 identifies and compares elements of health care systems under the traditional prepaid group practices' and medical care foundations' organizational models. Each of those elements will be discussed.

Unlike the traditional fee-for-service system, in both prepaid group practice and medical care foundations there is a formal management organization— the health plan. Health plan administrators arrange a delivery system, market its comprehensive services, and assume responsibility for a delivery system to provide the services promised. The prepaid group practice system plays a more active role in organizing the delivery system than does the medical care foundation which deals with the already-established, solo-practice system in the community.

While all three systems provide eligible people with similar comprehensive services, eligibility in both alternative systems is restricted to those enrolled in the plan.

In contrast to the payment for service at the time provided (or afterward)

TABLE 1 ■ Comparison of elements of health care systems

Elements	Fee-for-service	Prepaid group practice	Medical care foundations
System management	None	Health plan	Health plan
Consumers	Eligible persons	Enrolled eligible persons	Enrolled eligible persons
Payment	Fee-for-service	Capitation to plan	Capitation to plan
Physician:			
Organization	Various	Defined	Defined
Practice	Mostly solo	Group	Mostly solo
Reimbursement	Fee-for-service	Typically salaried	Fee-for-service set by plan
Accessibility to care	Marketplace access to providers	Assured access to providers	Assured access providers
Risk	Bad debts	Plan and providers share risk	Insurer and foundation share risk

of fee-for-service practice, the prepaid group practice plan takes the enrolled population's prepaid per capita premiums and allocates these monies (e.g., plans, budgets, controls, incentives, and protocols) to manage and finance the delivery system. Medical care foundations also are prepaid on a per capita basis, but since they contract with traditionally organized physicians, the foundation plan's ability to manage the delivery system is considerably lower.

All three systems use health care providers. Providers are formally organized in the alternative models. In the fee-for-service system, the providers are usually informally organized. Prepaid group practices typically emphasize some fairly cohesive form of group organization and group practice mode. Both fee-for-service and medical care foundations usually stress solo practice. Medical care foundation physicians are more formally organized than those in the fee-for-service system, but less so than in group practice. Prepaid group practices typically stress some form of physician reimbursement other than fee-for-service. In both fee-for-service and medical care foundations, fee-for-service is the reimbursement format; however, in medical care foundations, there is a negotiated fee schedule.

In both alternatives, enrollees are assured access to appropriate health care providers. In the traditional system, each eligible person shops in the marketplace for a provider who is ready, able, and willing to serve him.

In the fee-for-service system, individual physicians are at a risk after they provide the service—they may experience bad debts. In the alternative systems, the physician's organization is required to provide services over the year to the enrolled population whether or not the prepaid capitation payments are sufficient to cover the cost.

FROM GENETIC PRINCIPLES TO HMO STRATEGY: IMPLICATIONS FOR THE INNOVATION MANAGER

In the 1970s, the prepaid group practice movement was repackaged as the federal HMO program. The story of HMO politics and policymaking has been well described in Joseph L. Falkson's *HMOs and the Politics of Health System Reform*[24] and Paul Starr's *Public Interest* article, "The Undelivered Health System." Here I will interpret this story from the perspective of innovation management focusing on Dr. Paul Ellwood as an innovator. Our goal here is not to learn how Congress passes laws, but rather how managers make new things happen.

An innovation is born: A medical Moses who thinks like a Ford

In 1965, Dr. Paul Ellwood, a prominent pediatrician, was appointed head of the prestigious Minneapolis-based American Rehabilitation Foundation (will later be called Interstudy). Almost immediately he addressed a moral-practical dilemma: how could his institution do good—a la Moses—by rehabilitating patients to the point of self-reliance when this would end their payment to his institution for its services, threatening its economic survival? Ellwood needed to reorganize his institution to transcend this dilemma. The key that worked for him was Robert A. Levine's entrepreneurial theory of social strategy, which holds that government could avoid inefficient bureaucracies by manipulating the economic incentive structure in private markets to spur social problem solving. In this context, health care institutions misbehave because they are financially rewarded to do so.[25] The medical care organization trick, then, became how to economically reward health service organizations for keeping people healthy. Ellwood's Mosaic concern for health led him to think—a la Henry Ford—about efficient, industrial-like health care corporations (prepaid group practices and medical care foundations were his prototypes) for health care reform.[26] He raised a moral question like Shadid and answered it with organizational tinkering like Garfield.

Ellwood's analytic stress on economic incentives coupled with his moral concern for keeping people healthy led naturally to the prepaid group practice concept and genetic code. Ellwood then expanded this into a plan to reform all of American health care. In this process, however, the power of language and ideas encouraged Ellwood to come up with a mutation of this concept. Just as the genetic code of principles simplified the entrepreneurial realities of *creating* these local alternative delivery systems, he became mesmerized by one of these principles—the reversal of economics—at the price of oversimplifying the implementation challenge and ignoring the organization culture aspects of change.

The president as a patron in search of an innovation: Leadership—symbolic or substantive?

After wandering in the health policy desert for several years, Ellwood was finally called to Washington to describe his health care corporation idea for saving American health care. After a meeting with HEW bureaucrats who were familiar with prepaid group practice and had already initiated a small development effort, Ellwood went away disappointed. The bureaucrats filtered out his radical message that health care corporations should be the centerpiece for health care reform. As technicians, they simply noted that they had a prepaid group practice program in existence already.[27] He was making strategic policy points but they, as technicians, were simply replying in operational terms. Ellwood had approached managers who did not want to be innovation champions or agents. He had not yet communicated with someone in HEW who was strategically located and entrepreneurially minded enough to promote his innovation.

Finally, on February 5, 1970, Ellwood was invited by an HEW young Turk to meet with high HEW officials who were in a position to champion his innovation.[28] They had a dilemma of their own: how to react to the "health care crisis" in a politically advantageous way. The Democrats, led by Senator Kennedy, had used a delay in the Nixon administration's appointment of an assistant secretary of health to seize the initiative by constructing "the health care crisis" as a moral dilemma of social-medical justice calling for a New Deal type solution; that is, national health insurance (NHI).[29]

President Nixon, striking a leadership posture, had held a press conference on July 16, 1969, that was engineered to give the appearance of policy action on health care. He stated that the American health care system was not only in a crisis, but would actually break down in three years unless something was done to reform it. In describing the problem, he changed the terms of debating the issue by describing it as an economic crisis threatening health care's survival.[30]

The president, as innovation patron, needed a health reform concept. The administration, in an attempt to regain the initiative on this issue, assigned two top HEW nonhealth professionals—Californians John Veneman and Lewis Butler—to come up with a health care policy.[31] What is decisive here is that new health care policy was taken out of routine health profession–dominated channels and bureaus and located in the HEW secretary's office, which was stocked with a cadre of Ph.D.s, MBAs, and lawyer young Turks, one of whom acted as an innovation agent when he invited Ellwood to the meeting on February 5.

Champions import and transform the HMO innovation: The Pinocchio effect

On July 1, 1969, before a senate committee, Veneman discussed various reform ideas including prepayment, medical care foundations, group practice, and incentive reimbursement. Butler, in his charge to pull together a health policy proposal, suggested the need to frame it as a plan or strategy covering a certain span of time.[32]

At the following February 5 meeting, Ellwood presented his ideas, which had the same appealing kind of simple logic as the Laffer curve and supply side economics. Health institutions misbehave because they are paid to do so—we reward treating the sick, not keeping people healthy. Instead, we should set up prepaid group practice plans, like the Kaiser program, that offer rewards for keeping people healthy. What Ellwood suggested was consistent with both Veneman's and Butler's health care convictions and political agendas. Both were very familiar and impressed with the California-based, well-documented Kaiser prepaid group practice program. They thought in entrepreneurial terms. They served the president's political agenda.[33] Butler and Veneman were persuaded as convictions matched agendas.

Then Butler made one modification. He suggested that in keeping with a marketplace philosophy and Republican agenda, all specification of organizational structure should be omitted—let the marketplace decide. This was in keeping with Nixon's speech in which he changed the context of the health crisis debate from social justice to economic justice and from government intervention to marketplace competition. Ellwood, building on this idea, coined the term *health maintenance organization* using *health* to call attention to the emphasis on prevention, *maintenance* to affirm the emphasis on health promotion, and *organization* because it was a politically neutral word unlike prepaid group practice or corporation. They all agreed to focus on an HMO strategy as the core of the president's upcoming health message.[34] Supported by HEW Secretary Finch, Veneman and Butler championed the HMO innovation.

The Pinocchio effect then struck. The prepaid group practice movement had a history which offered evidence against which to test theory, and lessons upon which to implement sound programs. The transformation of prepaid group practice into HMO ripped the innovation out of historical context with some key distortions. First, Ellwood's overconfidence in economic incentives analysis screened out the importance of other key noneconomic PGP principles—for example, the central role of physician participation in administrative planning and budgeting. Second, whatever support prepaid group practice evidence gave to structural analysis theory was undercut when HMO was substituted for prepaid group practice in the strategy. There was meager evidence to support this appealing theory with respect to other forms of ADSs. Thirdly, over the years, prepaid group practice(s) had not provided all that much health promotion service. Fourth, the phrase "health maintenance" was not neutral, but provocative. It was coined by Dr. E. Richard Weinerman who used it to summarize a whole set of dilemmas raised by the kind of industrialization of health that Ellwood was advocating.[35] By making the innovation so diffuse, the stage was set for a boomerang effect. People, including opponents, could make of the HMO concept almost anything they wanted—both pro and con.

A yes-able proposal

Robert Fisher has suggested that an innovation advocate should negotiate in terms of "yes-able" proposals. In other words, he should understand the other party's interests, perspective, values, language, needs, and do as much of the work as possible (including that of the other party's staff) to form a proposal that takes this perspective into account while still selling the advocate's idea.[36] Ellwood and his staff made their HMO proposal yes-able. They did most of the work, they internalized the administration's perspective, and they wrote the proposal in the format that its users needed—a presidential message. This convinced Butler of the merits of both the proposal and its Interstudy drafters. He now had something on paper to champion, something to use to persuade his own people within HEW, and something to put on his patron's agenda.[37]

Implementation concerns lose out to ideological power-over politics

The paper became a lightning rod for debate. Career HEW bureaucrats challenged Ellwood's logic arguing that it would cost too much and would be hard to implement. The champions dismissed this as operational nit-picking at a bold strategic initiative. The document was refined, not to improve its workability, but to sharpen the ideological contrast of a self-regulating HMO industry versus an increased use of federal intervention by means of centralized planning and regulation.[38] Opposed by HEW career bureaucrats and screened by John Ehrlichman, the HEW champion's HMO proposal was not appealing to Nixon. He elected to delay a presidential health message and let HEW Secretary Finch carry the ball.[39] On March 25, 1970, Finch announced the HMO strategy.

Too much championing, too little patronage: Four basic implementation criteria get rediscovered

In June of 1970, Elliot Richardson replaced Finch as HEW secretary. On coming aboard, he discovered that the entrepreneurial mentality there had become so extreme that policy formulation was in a state of chaos— the young Turks were competing with each other and with the entrenched career health professionals. The HMO strategy had gotten lost in this "swamp." Richardson ordered a total review of policy. This lasted through December. The upshot was that Richardson emerged as a very aggressive champion of the HMO strategy encouraged by the young Turks who suggested that 5,000 to 10,000 HMOs be established. Aggressively, Richardson ordered a bootleg operation by which existing HEW resources would be reallocated to fund HMO projects while legislative action was being worked through. On February 18, 1971, Nixon delivered his health message with the HMO strategy at its center.[40]

HEW's bootleg HMO operation funded 79 projects before Congress stopped this unauthorized effort in January 1972. The effort was, in effect, a demonstration project. Four basic requirements—principles well established in the prepaid group practice movement—were rediscovered by the inexperienced HMO advocates about starting HMOs: a committed sponsor, physicians involved in the planning, effective management, and a reasonable estimate of market demand.[41] The year 1972 was a presidential election year. Nixon sharply curbed his interest in HMOs under pressure from the AMA. The

AMA made the debate claim that to promote HMOs would be unfair to their fee-for-service competition. Then, Richardson along with many young Turks left HEW. He was replaced by Casper Weinberger who redefined HMO as a mere experiment.[42] A champion was replaced by an innovation stifler.

One way of assessing how HEW had handled its HMO project is to apply the demonstration effort's findings to HEW management of the HMO initiative. First, Nixon, the patron, was not committed to developing HMOs. Second, key potential allies, such as physicians and other health professionals within HEW, were not involved significantly in the policy planning process. Third, although the innovation was strongly championed, it was not managed very well causing numerous administrative errors, staff changes, and so on. Fourth, little research was done about the market for HEW HMO grants. Street-level implementation concerns were simply ignored.

The HMO Act of 1973—Ideology wins over workability, and credibility suffers

The years leading up to the HMO Act of 1973 (Public Law 93–222) featured a disappearing act by the innovation patron. Although Nixon had begun the HMO debate in Congress, it was fought out among powerful Republican and Democratic congressmen. Ideological party politics overwhelmed practical implementation consideration. The product was overblown in terms of expectations and not workable in implementation. The law, for example, provided near total benefit coverage, but provided no subsidies to help these "white elephants" compete in the marketplace. The dual-choice provision, designed to give HMOs entree to consumers, was not implemented until two years later and hence confused both employers and employees, paralyzed marketing, and undermined HMO credibility in the private sector. Ignoring the challenging requirements of implementation, the act had the effect of eroding the credibility of HEW, HMOs, and of health reform in general. As Paul Starr observes,

> HMOs take years to develop. They require major infusions of capital and trained professional managers. Neither the capital or the management shells were readily available. . . . In view of the contradictory requirements of the legislation, the meager effort by HEW, the intrinsic risk in starting new business organization, and the lack of motivation in the industry to initiate HMOs or to cooperate with them, the slow development of HMOs in the mid-1970s should hardly have been a surprise.[43]

HMOs survive through consensus building and the feds turn HMO promoters

The period from 1974 to the present has been a turbulent time. Starting with the severe recession of 1974–75, there has been an overall reassessment of federal entitlement programs and a renewed emphasis on marketplace approaches to social problems. So HMOs have remained timely. Moreover, the HMO movement has made slow, steady progress in a stagnant economy.[44] At the congressional level, a remarkable lobbying group called "the Consensus Group" successfully worked to make the HMO law more workable.[45]

In 1979, the Carter administration came up with a more bullish HMO strategy—this time it was defined as one of business expansion with the government as an aggressive venture capitalist carving out attractive city markets across the nation ripe for HMO formation and market penetration. Ironically, it was a Democratic administration that first looked on the HMO movement as an emerging industry.[46]

At the 1979 GHAA Group Health Institute, Hale Champion presented the Carter administration's view of prepaid group practices and other HMO models. He criticized the Nixon administration's implementation of the HMO Act of 1973 and reaffirmed federal commitment to the movement:

> In 1971, President Nixon told you that by 1976 he wanted 1,700 HMOs with 40 million enrollees across the country. But what did his people do? They decided to treat HMOs as a demonstration program. They wrote regulations that most successful HMOs in the country couldn't qualify under, and they inhibited growth and development in a multitude of ways. We are through with this nonsense about demonstration. We are going to get about the business of stimulating the development of more HMOs—and we're going to stay in that business.[47]

Strikingly, HEW in the Carter administration not only accepted the HMO as a viable alternative, but used HMO experience to evaluate the traditional equilibrium. According to Champion, HEW used HMO performance in developing national health care policy:

> We found that HMOs offered a remarkable record of cost savings by reducing hospital admissions and lengths of stay. HMOs helped give us a basis on which to make some critical decisions. For we felt a lid of 9 or 10 percent increase on hospital revenues was reasonable, even generous, in light of the evidence that HMO members had only half as many hospital days per 1,000 members as Blue Cross/Blue Shield members. Clearly, fee-for-service hospitals had room to economize without undermining quality.[48]

Champion further noted that HMOs not only offer more efficiency, but they also offer access to the appropriate level of care and emphasize preventive medicine and quality care. Given these strengths, he stated that HEW would continue to strive to stimulate local groups to work together to plan and implement HMOs. At the close of his address, Champion called for a renewal of the enthusiasm and trust—the mutuality—that was characteristic of earlier voluntary action days in the prepaid group practice movement.[49] In short, he viewed prepaid group practice as part of a new and more voluntary health care framework.

Champion's talk was followed by an intensive HEW campaign to shift the HMO effort away from a bureaucratic approach toward a voluntary-action approach. HEW Secretary Joseph Califano set the tone at a 1978 HEW-sponsored HMO conference when he stressed the importance of a government-private sector problem-solving alliance to deal with the nation's health care crisis. He suggested that with the likelihood of NHI becoming reality, the HMO movement offered business and labor a last voluntary chance to tackle the task of containing health care costs. He urged corporate leadership to support HMOs at the local level. Finally, to help bring about better government-private sector cooperation, Califano announced the appointment of a former Ford Motor Company executive as an ambassador to help the business-labor sector promote HMO venturing.[50]

This HMO ambassador's role offers a clue to the nature of a voluntary-action alternative to a bureaucratic approach to change. Whereas a bureaucratic approach excels at defining desirable outcomes, it falls short in coping with the operational-process problems of attaining such outcomes. The HMO ambassador role reveals a renewed investment in dealing with the problems of innovation policy in implementation. This is good since *real policy is in its implementation.* Policy gets implemented and innovations get planned by means of marginal people—like the HMO ambassador—who work at the boundary between different sectors or cultures. This is the basic premise of the role innovator route to change.

This promotional posture towards the HMO movement has become central in the Reagan administration. The government will no longer fund new HMO initiatives but is promoting private, for-profit investment in the HMO movement, now characterized as a growth industry. This replaces a venture capitalist role for government in expanding voluntary sector-sponsored HMOs with a thrust to make the movement private.

THINK GLOBALLY BUT ACT LOCALLY

What is the lesson of the HMO movement from the 1970s? I believe that we learned that it is possible for the government to be a catalyst for voluntary health care reform when certain conditions are met, such as policy consensus, committed leaders, talented organizers, activated purchasers and payers, adequate capital, and the wisdom to learn the right lessons from past experience. The HMO movement has been misunderstood, advocated, and evaluated as a revolutionary approach to total health care reform, adequate in itself to win the war. The more sensible way to understand the HMO wars of the 1970s is to see HMOs as an example of guerilla warfare in a world of changing realities, where vanguard elements of the medical, hospital, insurance and consumer communities dissent from the status quo and band together in defensible enclaves. These new alliances build alternative health care institutions, which in turn pressure the general health care establishment to move in the same direction. HMOs are both health care rearrangements and, indirectly, pressurizers on more conventional institutions and professionals to similarly, but not identically, rearrange themselves into affordable health care systems in a turbulent world of changed realities. Increased competition in health care is a fact, survival is an imperative, and community service is a chosen responsibility.

Reflecting on the lessons that he has learned about health care politics in the 1970s, Dr. Ellwood has turned his attention to a voluntary approach emphasizing local action. He observes:

> I used to feel that there were some magic buttons in Washington. If they could be found and pushed, the medical care system could be transformed. But, I have literally given up the federal government as an effective change agent. I simply have not been able to change its basic ways whether it is controlled by politicians who share my reform philosophy or by people who oppose it . . . The health care system is a series of local enterprises. To change them, they must be taken one at a time, because each is different.[51]

This voluntary perspective stressing local diversity and initiative is precisely the one held by the Blue Cross organization in its 1970s HMO efforts. In the next section, we discuss voluntary local HMO action from the perspectives of the three health care groups—managers, providers and consumers. For it is axiomatic in negotiations that each involved party must understand the others' perspectives. In this section, we will see many of the survival curve principles at the local level, and pitfalls that appeared at the national level.

NOTES

Chapter 2

1. Ira Greenberg and Michael Rodburg, "The Role of Prepaid Group Practice in Relieving the Medical Care Crisis," *Harvard Law Review* 84, no. 4 (February 1971), p. 901.

2. Paul Starr, *The Social Transformation of American Medicine* (New York: Basic Books, 1982), p. 289.

3. Paul Starr, "The. Undelivered Health System," *The Public Interest* 42 (Winter 1976), p. 85.

4. George Perrott, *Federal Employee Health Benefits Programs: A Utilization of Services* (Washington, D.C.: HEW, 1971).

5. Odin W. Anderson, "All Health Care Systems Struggle Against Rising Costs," *Hospitals* 50 (October 1, 1976), p. 98.

6. E. Richard Weinerman, M.D. "Patients' Perceptions of Group Medicine Care," *American Journal of Public Health* June 1964, p. 833.

7. Committee on the Costs of Medical Care, *Medical Care for the American People* (Chicago: University of Chicago Press, 1932), p. 121.

8. George Rosen, M.D., "History and Health Care," *American Journal of Public Health* 67, no. 4 (April 1977), pp. 326–28.

9. Ibid., p. 327.

10. Paul Starr, *The Social Transformation,* p. 303.

11. Michael Shadid, M.D., *A Doctor for the People,* (New York: Vanguard Press, 1939), p. 305.

12. Starr, *The Social Transformation,* p. 302.

13. Samuel Moffat, "Kaiser-Permanente: Prepaid Comes of Age," in *1978 Medical and Health Annual* (Chicago: Encyclopedia Britannica, 1977), p. 124.

14. Greer Williams, "Kaiser," *Modern Hospital,* February 1971, p. 70. Also see Paul DeKruif, *Kaiser Wakes the Doctors* (New York: Harcourt Brace Jovanovich, 1943), p. 158.

15. Moffat, "Kaiser-Permanente," p. 126.

16. Raymond Kay, M.D., *Historical Review of the Southern California Permanente Medical Group* (Los Angeles: Southern California Permanente Medical Group, 1979), pp. 1–3.

17. Moffat, "Kaiser-Permanente," p. 126.

18. William A. MacColl, *Group Practice and Prepayment of Medical Care,* (Washington, D.C.: Public Affairs Press, 1966), pp. 25–35.

19. These principles abridged from Cecil Cutting, M.D., "Historical Development and Operating Principles," in *The Kaiser-Permanente Medical Care Program,* ed. Anne Somers (New York: Commonwealth Fund, 1971), pp. 19–21.

20. Richard Handschin, M.D., "Operating Principles of Group Health Cooperative of Puget Sound" presented at the Prepaid Group Practice School, Seattle, Washington, February 1972, p. 8.

21. Moffat, "Kaiser-Permanente," p. 129.

22. Starr, *The Social Transformation,* p. 321.

23. Moffat, "Kaiser-Permanente," p. 129.

24. Joseph L. Falkson, *HMOs and the Politics of Health System Reform,* (Chicago: American Hospital Association, 1980).

25. Ibid., pp. 13–16.

26. Ibid., p. 25.

27. Ibid., p. 25–27.

28. Ibid., p. 28.

29. Ibid., pp. 3–6.

30. Ibid., p. 6.

31. Ibid., p. 5.

32. Ibid., p. 9.

33. Ibid., pp. 28–31.

34. Ibid., pp. 31–32.

35. Weinerman, "Patients' Perceptions," p. 833.

36. Robert Fisher and William Ury, *Getting to Yes* (New York: Penguin Books, 1983), p. 82.

37. Falkson, *HMOs and the Politics*, pp. 34–35.

38. Ibid., pp. 38–39.

39. Ibid., p. 41.

40. Ibid., pp. 51–57.

41. Ibid., p. 83.

42. Ibid., p. 84.

43. Starr, *The Social Transformation*, p. 408.

44. Ibid., p. 405 and 415–16.

45. Falkson, *HMOs and the Politics*, pp. 175–84.

46. Ibid., pp. 193–94.

47. Hale Champion, "Keynote Address," presented at the 27th Annual Group Health Institute, Los Angeles, June 1922, 1977, p. 2.

48. Ibid., p. 3.

49. Ibid., p. 4.

50. Joseph Califano, remarks at HHS sponsored conference on HMOs, Washington, D.C., March 10, 1978.

51. Quoted in John K. Inglehart, "Health Care and American Business," *New England Journal of Medicine* 306, no. 2 (January 14, 1983), p. 124.

■3

The payer negotiates
the survival curve

PAYER MOTIVES FOR BECOMING ACTIVELY INVOLVED

Activating themes

■ Some health care purchasers and insurers—the payers—woke up in the 1970s to the health care cost problem. In the private sector, for example, William Goldbeck, director of the Washington Business Group on Health, called for renegotiating the traditional purchaser-provider alliance:

> Business and the medical providers can, and nearly always do, form a coopera-
> tive relationship. To have substance and durability, it must be based on the
> understanding that industry's role has changed from passive payer to *active*
> informed participant.[1]

Moreover, specific businesses began to stress local action. Caterpillar Tractor Company, for example, faced with spiraling health care costs, helped spearhead a cost containment coalition in Peoria, Illinois, based on the voluntaristic notion that interested local parties know more about Peoria's health care problems and prospects than experts in Washington, D.C. At the coalition's first session, someone stressed the necessity of local voluntary action: "If we in this room, or people like us, don't address this subject locally, then we deserve what we get if the folks in Washington, D.C., decide to try to fix our problems for us. In other words, if we don't do it, we know who will."[2]

Similarly, from the voluntary sector, Walter J. McNerney, speaking for the Blue Cross Association, stressed the need for local health care voluntarism to balance marketplace competition and government regulation. Over the years, while heading the association, McNerney was the overall cost containment patron. He put this in a positive context arguing that Blue Cross Plans must not only continue their traditional role, but must also serve subscribers "through *active* efforts to contain costs."[3] To this end, he and his successor, Bernard Tresnowski, have given steady, clear support to HMOs. This steadfast HMO patronage by some voluntary sector leadership is in marked contrast to the up-and-down public sector support over the years.

McNerney, while criticizing the meager evidence in support of grandiose reform theories, stressed that "the only continuing fact is that with a tightly organized alternative delivery system, we have reduction in hospital use."[4] McNerney saw Blue Cross HMO creation as part of Blue Cross's efforts to be part of the rapid evolution of American health care that began in the late 1960s. He used HMOs as an exemplary innovation. And indeed, Blue Cross Plans have been involved in scores of HMO and HMO-like projects since 1968—well before the Federal HMO Act of 1973 (Public Law 93–222).

During the 1970s, the general direction sketched out by McNerney was developed by Blue Cross Plan top management into five themes: leadership; innovation and competition, hospital growth, physician behavior and Blue Cross Plan-hospital collaboration.[5]

Leadership. Blue Cross Plans have found their niche in our society by providing a workable scheme to pay providers for services delivered to consumers. Purchasers, such as government, business, and labor, expect Blue Cross to keep the system workable—to be leaders in finding solutions to health payment problems. A loss of nerve on the part of health insurers would create a power vacuum which the federal government would likely fill with some form of a national health insurance scheme. As Dave Stewart, president of the Rochester Blue Cross Plan, has said:

> Major reforms in organization are needed because we are spending more and more scarce dollars and apparently getting less and less cost effectiveness in return. HMOs are one solution to this problem. They provide an unusual opportunity for us to demonstrate Blue Cross leadership. We can use our capabilities to improve old systems, create new systems, and for the first time in history, make a choice in health care programs available to consumers across the country. What better way to shape the future than through reasonable choice.[6]

Promote competition and innovation. This relates marketing and leadership. Traditionally, when prepaid group practices gain accounts, they also expect the employer to offer a traditional health insurance option, such as Blue Cross/Blue Shield—a dual-choice arrangement. The dual-choice mechanism acts as a relief valve for the employer; that is, if a few employees are unhappy with the principal insurer, they can exercise the dual-choice alternative and thus not force the employer to shift coverage of all employees from one insurer to another. Hence, dual choice helps insurers retain accounts. It is also a marketing tool for acquiring new accounts since under dual choice an employer can offer a second insurer's HMO option without giving up its traditional coverage. At the leadership level, society expects Blue Cross to respond to the felt need for relief from health care inflation by starting HMOs as innovative relief valves. As one Blue Cross HMO champion has argued:

> What the social critic and planner is asking Blue Cross and Blue Shield is that they build relief valves called alternatives to test the validity of traditional schemes versus innovative ones. I would like to think that Blue Cross and Shield is secure enough to participate in such an evolutionary test.[7]

Hospital growth. With mounting occupancy problems resulting from changing disease patterns, professional standards review organizations (PSROs), health system agencies (HSAs), and increased competition, hospitals seek ways to grow without expanding their bed supply. HMOs are one path in which hospitals can redirect their efforts and diversify into ambulatory care which helps increase referrals to their beds.

Change physicians' hospital usage behavior. Prepaid group practice HMOs recruit physicians whose conservative practice styles stress an avoidance of needless hospitalization. At the same time, HMOs structure economic incentives to reward this professional behavior. This tends to have a ripple effect among other physicians in the community which moderates their hospital usage.

Collaboration. Recently, John Griffith has offered an entrepreneurial survival course for Blue Cross/Blue Shield much like Chrysler's in that it stresses gaining competitive advantage by means of cooperative ventures. He suggests that the plans can thrive in the 1980s if they serve customer needs by becoming collaborative partners with selected nonprofit providers in forming new alternative delivery system arrangements.[8] He suggests that in a turbulent world, plans will survive by doing what they do best—having close provider relationships and arrangements that permit innovative capitation arrangements; that is, HMO-like approaches.[9] Given unpredictable circumstances, the plans must defend themselves through diversification in collaborative joint ventures with preferred providers; that is, those who want to control costs. Griffith identified HMOs as a prime example of this survival strategy.[10]

INTERNAL RESISTANCE TO CHANGE: THE BIGGEST OBSTACLE

Communities often expect large, established organizations like Blue Cross Plans to be innovators. Yet these organizations move slowly. Indeed, one Blue Cross prepaid group practice planner spoke for many when he said, "The toughest job I have is selling the people inside my own organization." The reason for this is simple—innovations pose, as Schon noted, the possibility of radical change in an organization and in its relationship to other organizations. For example, someone within an insurance or manufacturing company may begin talking about the direct provision of medical care services while someone within a hospital starts talking about carrying risk for peoples' use of beds. These are strange topics to others within those organizations whose task is not to develop new alternatives but to keep the established organization on track; that is, to maintain the old priorities, programs, and interorganizational relationships.

Innovations bring new opportunities, but they also bring new hazards. This challenge occurs within established health care organizations that plan to initiate prepaid group practices or other alternate delivery systems. Consider the question of market and business definition. When a health insurance company explores getting into an alternative delivery system, it is, in effect, expanding its definition of what business it is in. The insurance company expands its role from that of carrying the risk for illness payments to being more directly involved in the delivery of health care services. Similarly, when a hospital contemplates such a venture, it is with the goal of extending its role beyond that of providing inpatient facilities to making customer contact at the primary care level and getting involved in risk taking.

This redefining of an organization's business, market, or purpose is threatening to people who have dedicated much or all of their careers to successfully achieving the organization's traditional purpose. Someone is suddenly saying that there is an alternative that in some ways is better. Further, behind the label "alternative" is the threat that the innovation will expand and replace the traditional product and displace well-established organizational power centers.

These broad considerations lead to more specific problems concerning techniques and approaches. A health insurance company that launches a prepaid group practice plan must be prepared to change its traditional marketing approach to a stronger advocacy posture similar to that used in the 1930s and 40s by health insurance pioneers selling what were then innovative products—health care prepayment plans. Questions of approach raise questions of organization, skill, and responsibility. Should units of the traditional corporate hierarchy do the innovative job? Should a new unit be formed? If so, what will its relationship be to traditional units? How will this affect relationships with other organizations? Small wonder, then, that these innovative ventures meet with substantial resistance. How then do you organize for innovation?

ORGANIZATIONAL CULTURE ACTION PRINCIPLES

Organizing for innovation: The lessons of the CIO and Kaiser–Permanente

One way to survive into the future is to imitate the great organizers of the past. The labor and PGP movements offer two examples. The resistance of the American Federation of Labor (AF of L) in the 1930s to John L. Lewis' proposal for industry-based unions has some striking and informative parallels to the traditional health care field's reaction to prepaid group practice. Lewis is a prime example of a role innovator. His experience can tell us some important things about resistance to and organizing for innovation. He enlarged the role of the union organizer and thereby changed how the American labor movement evolved. His alternative view of organizing covered union mission, organization, marketing definition, and strategies.[11] He was a culture changer.

Like organized medicine, the federation was organized along craft lines. Lewis proposed an alternative—organizing systemwide by industry rather than by craft. Similarly, prepaid group practice unites all the aspects of personal health care services in one system. According to Lewis, the survival and growth of craft unions hinged on the creation of industrial unions (e.g., steel, auto) which could organize unorganized, unskilled workers. This parallels the prepaid group practice argument that its competition with fee-for-service medicine can benefit both itself and the traditional system. Moreover, in recruitment of members for both industrial unions and prepaid group practice, choice is the key. In the labor situation, Lewis worked for inclusion of Section 7A in the National Industrial Recovery Act of 1933, which mandated that workers have their choice of bargaining agent. Likewise, prepaid group practice proponents have sought state and federal legislation mandating that insured health care consumers have dual choice—a choice between traditional health care plans and one or more innovative options.

Leadership of the federation opposed Lewis on the grounds that his proposal would be too costly and that it would be a threat. He answered that it was worth the investment and was essential to the prosperity of traditional unions. Citing past failures in organizing industries, federation leadership contended that it was not possible to organize industries using traditional methods of organizing. Lewis agreed, but contended that it was possible if new principles of organizing were followed. Unable to win this debate within the federation, Lewis successfully started the Congress of Industrial Organizations (CIO) as an alternative union system.

Lewis' approach to innovative organizing had five basic elements:

Union leaders must have an enlarged and dedicated *sense of mission* for their self-interest to be served in the long run.

This overall purpose must be implemented by a *cadre of committed organizers.*

This cadre must follow *innovative practices of organizing.*

Organizers must be given adequate *money* to get the job done.

Organizers need *access to market* which requires that prospective members have choices.

Over the years, the AF of L and the CIO grew closer and finally affiliated. The relationship between traditional organized medicine and prepaid group practice has followed a similar evolutionary and, at times, rancorous path.

These industry organizing principles are found in the Kaiser prepaid group practice experience. Beyond calling attention to the need for adequate capital, local consumer demand, and not too much local provider resistance, a Kaiser leader stresses the cultural dimensions necessary for organizational success:

> A sufficient number of skilled managers and other specialists imbued with the Kaiser–Permanente philosophy and experienced in our form of organization and operation must be available.
>
> Physicians from our existing groups who are well versed in the fundamentals of group practice prepayment are needed.
>
> The most important element in a direct-service program is people—the physicians, administrators, and their supporting personnel.
>
> A new program must have the firm commitment of the leaders in our established regions and their enthusiastic and active support.[12]

It is worth emphasizing that these process principles stress *people*—a cadre of skilled champions and committed patrons—all sharing an entrepreneurial *philosophy* that takes into account provider *politics* and community *population*. Prepaid group practice formation, then, cannot be understood in terms of only structure or strategy. Peters' and Waterman's other Ss are essential ingredients to a mastery of the culture of health care innovation.

One pitfall: Blaming the innovation for the mistakes of innovators

Innovators ignore these implementation cultural principles—including these four Ps—at their own peril. Over the years these implementation points have been ignored. Some inept prepaid group practice developers blame the innovation when the real problem is their failure to use these well-established principles of innovation. In this regard, they are like the early federation leaders who also blamed the innovation rather than the implementers.

A prepaid group practice case in point—the Columbia Plan in Maryland built around the concept's formal characteristics—had a rough time breaking even financially. Its developers blamed the concept for the program's poor performance. They stated: "Overall, the experience suggests that the health maintenance organization movement has only modest ultimate potential as an option in health care delivery in the current economic milieu of American medicine."[13] The developers derive this conclusion from a theoretical discussion of the fit between today's medical economy and abstract prepaid group practice characteristics.

Overemphasis on the concept's technical attributes led the developers of the Columbia Plan to ignore well-established implementation principles. Roberts and Saward note:

As a traditional case history, the report of the Columbia Plan adds to our knowledge. It tells us that it is very difficult to develop a successful prepaid group practice if one locates in a sparsely populated area, depends for enrollment upon the residents of a new planned city, commits oneself to the expensive construction and operation of a hospital, involves a university that apparently had serious doubts about its involvement, and does not give substantial power to the medical providers.[14]

Roberts and Saward conclude that the developers of the Columbia Plan simply ignored well-established principles for implementing a prepaid group practice.[15] They failed to learn from past experience.

THE SURVIVAL CURVE MANAGER: CHAMPION, DEBATER, CONSENSUS BUILDER

Innovation champion

John van Steenwyk, a management consultant who has worked with scores of organizations striving to start prepaid group practice programs, suggests that, at the center of successfully developed programs, he has seen *innovation champions.* He observes:

Every alternative delivery system activity requires a single leader. Somewhere in every new program there is a responsible party—a guiding spirit, a sponsor, an innovator. This is essential. It is kind of like making honey: you can't do it without a queen bee. Hence—recognize that there must be such an essential creature. And make sure that there is scope for effective action and for incentives and rewards.[16]

To make this champion approach work, the organization's chief executive officer must be the champion's patron. Only someone at the top of the organization's hierarchy can have the formal and informal authority to be effective in protecting the champion from bureaucratic hostility to new concepts. In Blue Cross Plans, usually the plan president, if favorably inclined, acts as innovation patron. He may be more or less aggressive in this role. The vice president acts as innovation champion.

The health manager who champions an alternative delivery system (ADS) is in the import-export business. Positioned at his company's boundary, he imports new ideas into his organization and exports the plan's commitment. His territory is the interface between his organization and its environment. With this territory comes the problem of keeping imports and exports balanced. He must promote the alien innovation inside, but not to the point where he loses his colleagues' cooperation. Outside, he must cooperate with other groups, but not to the point where he fails to pursue his organization's interests. (Early in the face of the federation's intransigence, Lewis had great difficulty, as we have seen, with the import task. On the other hand, he had great early success and late failure in exporting commitment when he gained and then lost a crucial alliance with President Roosevelt.) This dual role requires a certain role innovator outlook—one that combines managerial and missionary skills. The champion is an advocate, not a zealot. He seeks and listens to advice.

Debate: Contexting plus pros and cons

Internally, the champion debates on behalf of the innovation, addressing the new realities of the marketplace. He raises questions such as: How will prepaid group practice affect the pivotal role of physician control of hospital usage? What about political pressure from local authorities and proponents of national health insurance (NHI) for established organizations to adapt and innovate? What about the need to shift hospital energies to ambulatory programs? The key to promoting the prepaid group practice concept internally requires building on these *external pressures*.

As communicator, the HMO champion must place the debate in a larger context—one that mixes dangers, necessities, and opportunities. Here are some arguments used by Blue Cross HMO proponents:

Entrepreneurship and survival

1. HMO development is a risk business. . . . Looking ahead to NHI, the brownie points will go to those Blue Cross Plans that are in there mixing it up, irrespective of who, in the long-run, "owns" the HMO. HMOs are best understood as NHI increments: largely unavoidable and undeniable responses to powerfully felt needs of employers for relief through innovation. HMOs are a way to retain our present accounts, acquire new ones, and assure a central place in any competition-oriented NHI scheme.[17]

Community service mission and survival

2. Blue Cross Plans are not insurance companies. They are non-profit, community service health care organizations. Their business is not solely hospital reimbursement. Their business is health and health services. What makes Blue Cross unique is public confidence. Preserving this confidence requires extending this tradition of concern about health, health services, and prepayment to the role of developing organized systems of care directly responsible for the provision of that care to an enrolled population of subscribers, to developing HMOs.[18]

Epidemiological necessity

3. Why today's concern with prepaid group practice, once the object of attention solely of health care enthusiasts? It results from a shift in the

kinds of diseases which cause the most problems and cost the most money. We have to contend with the fact that today, the main problems result from chronic and not acute diseases. Chronic conditions require organizing health systems that provide for continuity of care assuring access to appropriate services. HMOs are one proven alternative delivery system that incorporates these characteristics.[19]

Inevitable trend towards organized health care systems

4. Medical practice in America has gone through seven stages:
   a. Solo practice.
   b. Group practice.
   c. Integrated medical specialties on a group basis.
   d. Integrated medical specialties on a group basis, but with fees pooled to produce prearranged salaries for the physician.
   e. Integrated medical specialties on a group basis with no fees for services; rather a monthly charge to cover the cost of most or all medical needs.

PGP adds two stages:

   f. Same as e. but enrolling a known population at a monthly charge per head.
   g. Owning the hospital.[20]

These debate themes show how HMO champions draw attention to governmental and marketplace dangers and opportunities as well as the urgent need to adapt to unavoidable changes—the push of necessity. They all strive to present HMOs as having the winds of change at their backs. The law of the situation, to use Follett's phrase, calls for aligning one's organization with these basic shifts.

One way the innovation champion educates and gains the cooperation of his colleagues in entrepreneurial ventures is by answering their questions about and objections to the new concept. In seeking to gain their respect for his organizing activities, he must also respect their activities and more administrative viewpoints. He is an advocate who listens judiciously. Following is a list of illustrative objections to innovation and typical responses in the 1970s:

Debate con	Debate pro response
Cost:	
It will cost too much.	In the context of health care inflation, this competitive alternative will be worth the investment. It is a major cost-containment tool.
Risk:	
The risk is too great.	The risk to corporate survival if we do nothing is greater.

Debate con	Debate pro response
Compatability: This program is incompatible with our philosophical principles.	The alternative enlarges our corporate mission from just being for a certain product to providing our customers with whatever kinds of health care coverage or service they demand.
Threat: If we offer an HMO, we'll be competing with ourselves. This could replace traditional business.	This kind of competition is healthy. It maintains and expands our total business. Buick competes with Chevy and GM benefits—as does its customers. This is an alternative innovation that, as experience demonstrates, is a viable consumer option.
Workability: If this idea is so needed, how come some programs have failed and others find it hard going?	Some programs have failed because they used traditional approaches when new approaches to organizing for innovation are needed. These approaches are needed to transform felt need to active demand. Health care is a very personal service and acceptance of alternatives comes slowly but it has been demonstrated that innovative programs can succeed.

This debate is part of an organization's struggle to transform its internal culture to meet the demands of turbulent times. In the 1970s, some Blue Cross Plans strove to get on the survival curve and become more entrepreneurial. HMO participation was a way to learn about risk taking, getting closer to the customer, and innovating.

Consensus building

Although chief executive support is necessary, it is not sufficient for gaining internal organizational support. The innovation champion has to use formal and informal channels of communication and coordination to educate by debate and consultation those people whose cooperation he needs. Ronald Nick, while a Blue Cross HMO young Turk, described this consensual aspect:

> In thinking about the planning process and some of the lessons we learned, I am impressed with the extent to which we underestimated the complexity of the planning task and the need for greater institutional support. We learned quickly that a prepaid group practice program was far removed from our regular business. . . . Not only did we have to work with the outside provider world on an equal basis, but we had to internally develop a set of systems and procedures to meet specific subscriber and provider needs.[21]

Hence, innovation planning needs to spend more time on planning and consensus building *prior* to decision making and implementation.

THE COOPERATIVE MIND-SET

Effective entrepreneurial action and innovation championing require, as Nick suggests, not only collaborative internal relationships, but also cooperative external relationships. Prepaid group practice entrepreneurship requires both the ability to debate and the ability to compromise. Management cannot unilaterally produce a marketable medical program. Managers must relate not only to each other, but to hospitals, physicians, and consumers as well. This flows from the very nature of a prepaid group practice—it directly intertwines defined sets of managers, providers, and consumers into a closed system.

Hence, the innovation champion must have a cooperative mindset in order to build a system based on a tight mutuality of interest. For example, no prepaid group practice can complete its planning and then expect a physician leader to join the program like an assembly line employee. If physicians are to accept a prepaid group practice plan—where they will be the central producers—they will be expected to be full partners in the planning activity.

Dr. William A. MacColl, a leading authority on the PGP movement, claims that a cooperative outlook is the key to program success. Innovation planners must want "a system of care and coverage responsive to both the health needs of [their] community and to the professional needs of physicians."[22] According to MacColl, a crucial step in program planning was to offer physicians the opportunity to work together *with* rather than *for* consumers. This power-with approach demonstrates a genuine commitment to the formation of a joint venture.[23]

This cooperative point of view in successful entrepreneurial programs runs through their planning, development, and management phases. MacColl holds that this shared cooperative point of view, with its parallelism of consumer, physician, and manager interest, forms a unique partnership "in planning, serving, and supporting each other [which] has no equivalent in [traditional] medical economics."[24] An essential aspect of this unique form of partnership is that the actors each have a specific problem-solving style. Organization culture mechanisms must be developed to ensure that people of different but cooperative viewpoints can meet around a table and work on a problem of mutual interest.

Finally, MacColl concludes his assessment of prepaid group practice entre-preneurship by stressing the importance, not of abstract innovative concept but of concrete *interpartner process:*

> While there are many differences in the detailed structures of the various admin-istrative organizations in GHAA [Group Health Association of America], there are now enough thoroughly proven principles of consumer health plan adminis-tration to guide the organizers of a new plan away from most of the shoals. It is neither the size, the complexity, nor the structure of an administrative pattern that makes it work. It is the people.[25]

Cooperative planning must foster the growth of this power-with process. It strives to collaboratively establish governance and management capabilities which can develop the policy principles and the administrative and health care delivery systems necessary to accomplish community-oriented health care goals. The solution, then, is not in the structure or system—it is in the local change process and its people.

COLLABORATIVE PRINCIPLES FOR INNOVATING BY NEGOTIATION AND COMPROMISE

Prepaid group practice experience provides some straightforward ground rules on how interpartner mutuality is sought and kept by manager, provider, and consumer planning participants. These cooperative rules are useful to both internal and external collaborative planning.[26] They are the method of moving from debate to compromise.

Leadership—Each group needs an identified champion who clarifies the group's self-interest in light of their vision of the program's overall purpose; translates and communicates this interest and vision to the other allies; translates and communicates other views back to his group; and negotiates with his group's allies.

Hardheaded negotiations—Negotiations will be hardheaded since diverse interests in one common effort are involved.

Manageable crises—Crises are a normal part of the process and can be managed. These crises are used to ensure that each group's concerns are recognized and real issues of power are addressed.

Free discussion—Negotiation as the prime method of planning, innovating, and problem solving can have constructive outcomes when any subject can be raised; discussion proceeds on a shared fact base; all allies do their homework before meetings; there is a culture of trust and mutual respect; and when mutuality is sought and either/or proposals are avoided.

What must be done—Mutuality is sought with the knowledge that the new venture is too important to let fail. Hence, participants feel that good faith debate is essential for integrative compromises. The process, then, has a framing sense of necessity and fairness.

Pluralism—The negotiating parties recognize that they each have different and legitimate ideals and problem-solving perspectives and need to have a continuing role in the sense of identity in negotiated programs. This is essential in coalition building.

Innovating by negotiation, then, is a voluntary method that recognizes self-interests and seeks to find common purposes. It assumes both conflict and its collaborative resolution. It keeps the law of the situation in mind.

These prepaid group practice lessons on collaborative innovating are consistent with Rosabeth Moss Kanter's recent findings on the central role of managers in business innovation. She found that commercial companies succeeded in innovating by promoting a culture that fostered cooperation and a structure that encouraged managers to do what needed to be done. This collaborative culture, combined with a flexible structure, encouraged an entrepreneurial mentality.[27] Indeed, the lessons learned by New York City Blue Cross's Ron Nick are the same consensus and coalition-building lessons learned by entrepreneurial middle managers in general. Kanter identified five principles of participatory-collaborative management:

> Persuading more than ordering, though managers sometimes use pressure as a last resort.
> Building a team, which entails among other things frequent staff meetings and considerable sharing of information.
> Seeking inputs from others—that is, asking for ideas about users' needs, soliciting suggestions from subordinates, welcoming peer reviews, and so forth.
> Acknowledging others' stake or potential stake in the project—in other words, being politically sensitive.
> Sharing rewards and recognition willingly.[28]

The point here is that a middle manager can often succeed at innovating even as he moves to motivate top managers to become his patrons.

PREPAID GROUP PRACTICE CREATION AS COMMUNITY ENTREPRENEURSHIP: A POWER-OVER EXAMPLE

The prepaid group practice entrepreneur moves in a turbulent world where shifting external pressure makes corporate "foreign affairs" a central aspect of new program development. This is true to such an extent that program planning and implementation can be understood as a community political decision-making process. The experience of the Genessee Valley Group Health Association (GVGHA)—Blue Cross Plan-sponsored HMO in Rochester, New York—highlights this process and shows the hazards of innovation planning by power-over political compromises in Follett's sense of unworkable solutions. The Rochester prepaid group practice had a difficult start-up period. Analysis shows that the problem was poor implementation arising from ideologically intense community political decision making. The five steps of local HMO politics are discussed below.

Impetus for an actionable proposal

The process begins when an established, strategically placed organization and potential prepaid group practice organizer, such as a health insurance company or a medical group, senses a change in its environment—often a shift in its market—and considers prepaid group practice along with several other alternatives. Then, such initial investigations become crystallized into a proposal for action as *external pressures* become focused. In Rochester, New York, the impetus for change came from an organized business coalition. Its director was a role innovator who took the coalition deep into health care reform and made it, in effect, a path-breaking business health coalition:

> The initial spark for Genessee Valley Group Health Association came from Rochester's Industrial Management Council, a nonprofit service group composed of companies that employ about 90 percent of the area's manufacturing force. In 1968, the council's newly installed general manager, John Hostulter, galvanized concern over rising health care costs by focusing attention on the Blue Cross/Blue Shield 10-year premium projections for local industries: Kodak's hospital bill, for example, would jump from $5 million to $15 million without any change in benefits. The council asked Hostulter to look into the problem further.[29]

After creating an urgent sense of economic crisis, Hostulter explored the matter with local Blue Cross/Blue Shield Plan executives, comprehensive health planners, and various industrial leaders. In Rochester, Blue Cross was expected to take the lead. The consensus was that some form of alternative delivery system would be a constructive response to the cost problem. The prepaid group practice format specifically seemed promising. Diffuse concern was thus translated into a known innovative concept. This gave action a definite direction. Hostulter then acted much as Ellwood had in Washington— he instigated local actors into action.

Who decides?

Decisions about organizing new health care programs do not, however, happen in a vacuum. They are made in the context of a community's political culture and power structure; that is, the network of organizational arrangements and beliefs that control or influence how local resources are allocated. In Rochester, this structure is remarkably simple—a few corporate giants such as Kodak, Xerox, Sybron, and GM have provided a tradition of progressive business leadership in health planning. In fact, Rochester business leaders played a key role in establishing one of the nation's first Blue Cross Plans in the mid-1930s. Hostulter's explorations with these executives led not only to a shared desire to promote alternative delivery systems in Rochester, but also to the creation of a broad-based committee—including labor, business, Blue Cross/Blue Shield, and hospital and physician representatives—to do this promotion. Thus, a decision-making vehicle—the committee—was established to consider alternatives. This, in itself, is a key decision because the decision-making vehicle, as we will see, shapes how the ultimate decisions will be handled.

Deciding

In the case of New York's Genessee Valley, the broad-based committee gave alternative delivery systems legitimacy, but at the price of adding substantially to the number of people and interest groups involved in the decision-making process. Consensus of opinion was, therefore, harder to achieve. When the committee first began its deliberations about prepaid group practice plans, no other alternatives were discussed. Other options surfaced as an antiprepaid group practice ploy. Here we can see how the ideological resistance to the alternative innovation can affect innovation decision making and shape how it is designed, implemented, and tested.

Organized medicine—unhappy with the prepaid group practice concept— advocated a medical care foundation alternative which had the ideologically favored, solo practice, fee-for-service characteristics. Although the committee's industrial leaders agreed on the desirability of a prepaid group practice, they had not agreed on how to resolve conflict with the physicians. A compromise was reached whereby the committee agreed to endorse the medical care foundation (a competitor to its own alternative) in exchange for the medical society's endorsement of the prepaid group practice program. In retrospect, the Kodak representative recalls that it was just three business leaders who arrived at this power-over, dominated compromise. This resulted from the decision to go with a broad-based, decision-making vehicle which gave the county medical society veto power.

Implementation

Decision making about the choice of alternative also addresses how alternatives are to be implemented. The consequences of the Rochester compromise were that the committee not only recommended that both the prepaid group practice and the foundation programs be started and endorsed but also that the Blue Cross and Blue Shield plans handle marketing for all three alternatives, as well as for their traditional offerings—and do so in an impartial manner. The ideological debate point made by the medical society was that to advocate ADSs would be "unfair" competition. Moreover, one company insisted on doing its own marketing of these alternatives to its workers. It did so in an impartial fashion. At the time, the prepaid group practice's assistant executive director, who headed its marketing effort, had doubts about whether such a neutral approach could work.[30] Ideological community politics and industrial pride in its marketing expertise, however, outweighed technical implementation considerations. The impartial marketing campaign's upshot was an enrollment debacle. As Neustadt would say, the committee decided more than it had to at this point and thereby impaired implementation.

Evaluation and adjustment

Initially, the prepaid group practice program was faced with enormous losses because of poor enrollment which led to a substantially underutilized medical staff and health center. Just as Congress produced an unworkable HMO act that needed to be fixed, the Rochester committee designed a local HMO strategy that was designed for failure. At this point, the HMO's executive director and champion persuaded his patron, the Blue Cross CEO, that the marketing strategy needed to be fixed—that a workable compromise was necessary. The program's administrators decided to market the program on its own. In turn, the city's major companies accepted the necessity of this action.

Enrollment has grown rapidly since then, but a GVGHA continuing problem is amortizing its huge start-up costs—$3.6 million. At least $1.2 million of that debt resulted from having to deal with the foundation, which went out of business due to enormous problems.

No one was ever really happy with the compromise produced by the broad-based, decision-making process. The lesson to be learned from the Rochester experience is that while community pressure can be quite productive in unlocking a community's energies and opening the way for innovation, it may not be equipped to deal with the technical challenges of planning and implementing the innovation. The Rochester industrialists went beyond unlocking the situation for innovation—they relocked the innovation into an unworkable arrangement. This produced the costly irony of impartially marketing naturally competitive alternatives.

A POWER-WITH PROCESS: PREPAID GROUP PRACTICE CREATION AS ROLE NEGOTIATION

Technical and political processes can be amalgamated into a power-with approach to health care innovating as a community role negotiation process. In this approach, the actors who make up the local voluntary sector sort out when who does what. Typically, role negotiations follow a three-step process: First, the various concerned parties clarify the need for action and identify promising alternatives. Second, after clarifying the issues involved, they seek an initial solution on some specific common goal which involves a conceptual breakthrough or integrative idea. Third, they negotiate hard by giving content to the integrative breakthrough to see if the conceptual compatibility of roles is workable.

Using this three-step scheme, we can discern a similar three-stage process of role negotiation in PGP planning. First comes clarification, in which the involved parties investigate various innovative delivery system concepts. They clarify the concepts' applicability to the local community and the parties involved. The parties ask questions, such as: What is prepaid group practice? Is it desirable in our unique community? What will be our role in such a venture?

Next comes integration, where those parties that continue in the process jointly build a common fact base. By this cooperative action, the parties see that for a successful program to be planned, they must tailor a version of the general prepaid group practice concept that is politically and technically workable for their community. The question here is: What technical and political considerations and contraints will affect implementation of a viable program here?

In the third stage of workable roles, insurer-provider role negotiations take place. At this time, each side tests the other by making reasonable demands that cause the other side to be responsive or to withdraw. If these adjustments are mutually responsive, the basic questions are: Who has which roles, responsibilities, rewards, and risks in the proposed venture? Is this workable? Can we work together after the program starts? Since the overall process takes considerable time (from one to five years), the legal (state and federal) environment shifts, and local negotiation of roles correspondingly must be adjusted to these environmental changes. A workable set of roles emerge.

The process briefly described above can be broken down into a number of steps, many of which are illustrated by the experience of Blue Cross Plan developed prepaid group practice programs in New York City and Cincinnati.

Clarification

A large health care organization, such as a health insurance company, detects a shift in its environment and detects a demand for innovation. It then selects an innovation champion to explore possible future health care directions and to identify the most promising innovation in terms of local community needs and ideals. Other local groups—providers, purchasers, or consumers—also explore various health care innovations. In the case of Cincinnati, for example, organized labor's demand for a prepaid group practice provoked early consideration of that option.[31]

Community pressure for an innovation can be reinforced by two nonlocal forces. First, the potential innovation entrepreneur is often influenced by national forces, such as spokesmen for the federal government, foundations, or trade associations, such as the Blue Cross Association. Second, a working example of the innovation in the community's vicinity can be a powerful regional inspiration to experiment locally. Kaiser's presence in Cleveland was a spur throughout Ohio. As the champion's focus closes onto one solution, opposition emerges. Once he identifies the most promising option, he then organizes to study it intensely, often by forming an internal task force. By involving other people in innovation classification, he hopes that this process will help educate them about the innovation and increase their commitment to it; that is, he strives to build an effective innovation team. Often, such a participatory process will reveal that money and operating principles are not enough—that the right people, a collaborative process, and a conducive organizational culture are also vital for successful implementation. Ronald Nick's year-long period of investigation led to identification of some of the essential ingredients for local voluntary prepaid group practice collaboration:

> We began to understand the different types of programs and the advantages and disadvantages each might have for our particular environment. . . . There was no common blueprint for developing or insuring the success of a prepaid group practice venture. Success came in those places where there was a nucleus of knowledgeable, committed people working with sufficient financial support. Commitment and the ability of these people to work across institutional lines towards a common set of goals were the factors that made for success.[32]

The upshot of this investigation and period of free discussion is a position paper which persuasively champions the innovation by mapping out its underlying cultural and operating principles and mechanics. The paper relates the innovation's promise to the organization and to its culture. This presentation is supported by facts and figures from relevant research.

Integration

When the paper is persuasive, the process moves on to the next step. The champion is strategically located at the intersection of pressures—internal, purchaser, and provider. He sets up a process of interaction in which the various parties can evolve a shared understanding of what must be done. Task forces are established, and political and technical considerations are made to check one another. In Cincinnati, for example, hospital considerations were orchestrated to help produce compatible roles. The impetus came from organized labor which demanded that a prepaid group practice program be created. It brought in experts from the Kaiser–Permanente program—a prepaid practice approach which typically builds new hospitals. The Blue Cross Plan people debated the merits of the Kaiser approach's applicability to the Cincinnati situation. Shifting to a leadership role, the plan then suggested an integrative solution—working with some local hospital ally to create a prepaid group practice through local voluntary action. The plan, then, had accepted the necessity of creating a prepaid group practice in Cincinnati. The innovation champion had used external pressure to internally persuade top management to head the "inevitable" PGP parade.

From a marketing point of view, this provider-based approach is technically sound—consumers will opt for an alternative backed by a prestigious local hospital. It is also politically sound—local provider opposition will be reduced if a powerful provider plays a central role. During this phase, there must be the integrative realization that prepaid group practice formation is not a power-over effort and that a key ingredient for success is working with a well-respected provider to develop the program's medical component. Blue Cross in Cincinnati sought four things in its medical ally: management and leadership capability; understanding and commitment to prepaid group practice; an excellent reputation in the health care field (viewed as essential to recruiting the medical staff and sometimes vital to recruiting subscribers); and desirable geographical location in the right market area.

Finding a provider partner is not easy. A physician may be recruited to form a free-standing medical group as was the case in Rochester. The insurer-entrepreneur may choose a hospital to create the group practice, which happened in Cincinnati. There the role negotiator set up a process of contact, consultation, and education to instigate local interest in the concept. This was a long and frustrating process. The medical staffs of hospitals are often more conservative than their administrations or boards. Sometimes the role negotiator can help hospital management deal with internal restraints; that is, can help manage a crisis in the process. This was the case in the New York City experience where the chief executive of the Blue Cross Plan—the HMO patron—helped persuade a hospital board to patronize a prepaid group practice venture. In other cases, the role negotiator has to wait out intrahospital politics. This happened in Cincinnati. An insurer can potentially contribute management, access to market, and money to match a hospital's physician manpower. The role negotiator is the maverick that brings these four Ms—management, money, market, and manpower—together at the right moment.

Task force involvement with external allies is paralleled by further internal task force work and team building. For example, once a specific provider is selected, the insurer's marketing people are assigned to measure the feasibility of the specific program proposed.

Workability

Where roles are successfully conceptualized and found to be attractive, insurer-provider negotiations start. Their aim is to hammer out a set of workable program roles, rewards, responsibilities, and risks. The parties agree on general operational principles that provide an overall cooperative framework or purpose. This makes subsequent disagreement over means to achieve ends resolvable in constructive ways. Nick remarks:

> We agreed that the program should be sold with a community rated premium that combined both medical and hospital services. Secondly, we agreed that a single organization should take responsibility for providing or arranging for delivery of these relatively comprehensive services and be at risk for a predetermined capitation. Thirdly, that services should be delivered in a group practice setting in a single location.[33]

General principles are vital because in prepaid group practice ventures, all potential allies are negotiating in unfamiliar territory. Stress can get quite substantial. General agreement as to purpose and operating principles allows the innovation to evolve in dynamic negotiation. Shared principles are continually re-invoked throughout the planning process as specific issues—such as benefit design, marketing tactics, premium rates—are negotiated. While the debate tactics of each side are important—the insurers assert financial facts, the physicians assert professional ethics—the emerging cooperative culture is the key to evolving a new program that is viable. Overemphasis on debate tactics can lead to stalemates or power-over concessions that significantly weaken the innovation's design and, in turn, performance. For example, a provider may bargain so as to avoid risk for hospital utilization. This dilutes the innovation's operating principles and raises the question: How will hospital utilization be controlled? If there is no significant answer, the program will fail. Roles will have to be renegotiated after the validity of the physician risk and responsibility principle has been locally and painfully established.

Negotiations are usually carried out within a formal mechanism, such as a joint conference committee or task force. Crucial to the success of such a mechanism is constant and clear communication that can lead to a close working relationship among the role negotiators. In these negotiations, there is a constant testing of the other side's responsiveness and its willingness, say, to step out of its insurer perspective and see things from the point of view of the physicians—and to compromise based on this appreciation of the other side's needs, perspective, stake, and restraints. Negotiations are, then, cross-cultural. Role negotiations can take two or three years to fall into place. Meanwhile, the legal environment may well be undergoing some change. New state and federal laws could have been passed or old laws may have been modified. Hence, the outcome of role negotiations typically goes through another cycle as adjustments—often difficult ones—are made to these turbulent regulatory changes.

COMMUNITY HEALTH CARE COALITION-BUILDING BASICS: DEFINITION, COALITION, ACTIVATION, AND EMPOWERMENT

The business health coalitions that have sprung up around the country in the 1980s have made mistakes. They have learned lessons similar to those of the prepaid group practice experience a decade ago in such places as Rochester and Cincinnati as well as some new lessons. In 1981, a Des Moines, Iowa, business leader, for example, played much the same champion role that Hostulter played in Rochester. He looked at skyrocketing health care costs and identified a problem in need of a solution. As in Rochester, a small group of business leaders formed a broadly representative coalition to attack the problem with the same result. Organized medicine fought against starting an HMO. Moreover, business leaders who were hospital trustees remained loyal to their hospitals and the status quo rather than to their commitment to cost containment.

As was the case in Cincinnati, labor in Iowa proved a very strong ally in support of prepaid group practice creation. Strong, committed business innovation patrons, in the view of local coalition leaders, are decisive in making change happen. There are three barriers to gaining CEO participation: health care reform is a "dirty project" that upsets personal relationships in a community's power structure; HMOs are sometimes perceived ideologically by businessmen as something governmental and even socialistic; and health coalition and HMO building are risky ventures. Some CEOs may want to avoid the possibility of being a "loser" at health care reform.[34]

The Iowa experience offers an exciting lesson in the creative use of the media in supporting health care reform. While coalition efforts to create an HMO were proceeding, the Public Agenda Foundation was conducting Health Vote 1982. This was a communitywide effort to inform the Des Moines citizenry through the media about the urgent public policy issues in health care. The campaign culminated with a ballot poll conducted in the fall of 1982. Of the 30,000 ballots mailed in, 70 percent contained positive votes for HMO development. This was about a 50 percent increase in public approval for HMO action over precampaign levels. Clearly, community health care coalitions need to seriously consider this new political tool.[35] The Des Moines HMO was launched in 1983.

It is useful to understand the Des Moines experience in terms of Rosabeth Moss Kanter's view of entrepreneurial innovation which parallels Bolan's and Aiken's ideas. She suggests that successful innovations follow a three-step process—definition, coalition, and activation. She notes that in the first step, innovators sense new problems and suggest new approaches to solving them. In the coalition step, the innovators build an alliance to marshall support from the whole involved culture. This requires considerable political savvy. The final step is implementation, which demands continued efforts to persuade, motivate, and maintain commitment.[36] Adapting her intraorganizational ideas to a communitywide enterprise, a Des Moines business leader defined an issue, built an alliance to attack it, and maintained momentum in the face of stiff opposition. The result was seeing the proposed HMO solution launched.

Moreover, it is not enough to initiate an innovation. Patrons and champions must work to make the innovation succeed in the marketplace. Kanter believes that managers can create environmental conditions that allow innovations to flourish. This cultural transformation occurs through people empowerment; that is, the capacity to mobilize people (and things) to get new things done. Crucial to empowerment is a free flow of information where innovating coalitions disseminate information on needs and problems in order to stimulate realistic, innovative problem solving.[37] Health Vote 1982 is an example of this fourth innovation step, empowerment.

Walter J. McNerney, reviewing the emergent business coalition movement including the Des Moines experience, offers the following negotiation, coalition-building guidelines:

Expect no simple answers since health care is so complex.

Involve all relevant interests.

Strive for mutual respect and commonality of purpose.

Participants must be authorized to make commitments.

Proposed strategies should reflect local characteristics and history.

Goals should be positive and not polarizing.

Build a sense of community.

The coalition should play a catalyzer, not implementor, role.

Health care leaders should, in turbulent times, recognize the need for selected, community-oriented, collaborative enterprises.

Hospital trustees should enter into such enterprises where they serve the hospital's community obligation of improving the public's health status.[38]

The point here is that the creation of competitive health care innovations requires institution and agreement building. Coalition action is essentially a venture in social entrepreneurship requiring all the tools of survival curve management.

THE MANAGER AND THE INDUSTRIALIZATION OF HEALTH

Once an innovation becomes operational, the program's workability gets tested. Mistakes made along the way in planning and development become obvious once the program is underway. They can, for example, result in high operating losses. The developers are tested in their common role of innovation champion. An insurer, for example, can seek to compensate for unanticipated losses by driving the prepaid innovation's premiums up, but this could well reduce enrollment and seriously impair the young program before it gains local consumer recognition as a valid option. When the sponsor prematurely asks the innovation to be self-sufficient, the stage is set to blame the concept for program failure when it is actually the inept application of well-known implementation rules that creates poor performance.

Another consequence of launching an innovation is that the sponsors face new issues. Labeling prepaid group practices as health maintenance organizations raises new questions. Elliot Richardson eloquently raised the health maintenance issue as health care became thought of as an industrial production system:

> With the desirable modification of incentive systems so as to encourage greater efficiency—for example, in the development of health maintenance organization—these pressures will only be reinforced.
> But, the question gnaws over whether we, as a society, are now . . . as inventive in our quest for qualities of personalism and immediacy as we are in our very necessary quest for efficiency; whether in our race to an industrial revolution in health we are inventive enough to insure that the best of the old order is preserved . . . in the new.[39]

Buried in the term *HMO* is the question of whether organizations can promise health. HMOs are often conceptualized in corporate and management terminology as if health can be promised by systems in the same way mail is delivered by the postal system. Health, however, is not a deliverable product but a personal, communal, and environmental balance. Health service is, at its root, a one-to-one relationship.

NOTES

Chapter 3

1. Quoted in Ronald A. Hurst, "What Does Management Think Should be Done About Containing Health Care Costs," *Health Care in the American Economy:*

Number 3, ed., David H. Klein and John F. Newman (Chicago: Blue Cross and Blue Shield Associations, 1980), p. 51. (Italics added)

2. Ibid., p. 55.

3. Walter J. McNerney, "Containing Health Care Costs," in Klein and Newman, *Health Care*, p. 61. (Italics added)

4. Ibid., p. 64.

5. Paul Young, remarks at the Blue Cross Association Annual Board Meeting, Chicago, 1974.

6. Dave Stewart, "The HMO Challenge," paper presented at the Blue Cross Association HMO Marketing Conference, Dallas, 1976, p. 3.

7. Paul Young, letter to the author, January 25, 1976.

8. John R. Griffith, "The Role of Blue Cross and Blue Shield in the Future U.S. Health System," *Inquiry*, Spring 1983, p. 18.

9. Ibid., p. 16.

10. Ibid., p. 18.

11. See generally, Saul D. Alinsky, *John L. Lewis* (New York: Vintage Books, 1970), pp. 60–80.

12. Anne E. Somers, ed., *The Kaiser–Permanente Medical Care Program* (New York: Commonwealth Fund, 1971), pp. 155–158. Abridged.

13. Robert M. Heyssel, M.D., and Henry M. Seidel, M.D., "The Johns Hopkins Experience in Columbia, Maryland," *New England Journal of Medicine* 295, no. 22 (1976), p. 1225.

14. James Roberts, M.D., and Ernest Saward, M.D., "Letter to the Editor," *New England Journal of Medicine* 296, no. 10 (1976), p. 578.

15. Ibid., p. 578.

16. John van Steenwyk, "The Insurer Role in HMO Planning and Development," paper presented at the Blue Cross Association Conference on Alternative Delivery System Planning, New Orleans, 1975, p. 3.

17. Young, letter.

18. van Steenwyk, "The Insurer Role," p. 1.

19. Ibid., p. 2.

20. Paul Young, "Special Report: Prepaid Group Practice," (Cincinnati: Blue Cross, 1972), pp. 1–2. Abridged.

21. Ronald M. Nick, "Cooperative Planning—The Alternative Delivery System Coordinator Point of View," paper presented at the Blue Cross Association Conference on Alternative Delivery System Planning, New Orleans, 1975, p. 3.

22. William A. MacColl, *Group Practice and Prepayment of Medical Care* (Washington, D.C.: Public Affairs Press, 1966), pp. 1–2.

23. Ibid., p. 169.

24. Ibid., p. 184.

25. Ibid., p. 187.

26. Aubrey Davis, Jr., "Interaction of Board with Medical Staff and Administration," paper presented at Group Practice School, Seattle, 1972.

27. Rosabeth Moss Kanter, "The Middle-Manager as Innovator," *Harvard Business Review,* July–August, 1982, pp. 95–96.

28. Ibid., p. 102.

29. "Genesee Valley Group Health Association," in *The Complex Puzzle of Health Care Costs* (Washington, D.C.: President's Council on Wage and Price Stability, 1976.) The following interpretation is based largely on this excellent case study.

30. Raymond Savage, "Marketing," in *Proceedings of the 24th Annual Group Health Institute,"* Washington, D.C., 1974, p. 5.

31. The material here on Cincinnati draws upon Paul Young, "HMO Cooperative Planning," presented at the Blue Cross Association Conference on Alternative Delivery System Planning, New Orleans, 1975. I also appreciate Paul Young's help in my preparing a fuller unpublished case study of this experience.

32. Nick, "Cooperative Planning" p. 3.

33. Ibid., p. 4.

34. See both John K. Inglehart, "Health Care and American Business," *New England Journal of Medicine* 306, no. 2 (1982), p. 124; and "Business is Re-learning Its ABCs," *Perspective,* Spring 1982, p. 33.

35. "HMO Network in Des Moines Set for Summer," *Group Health News,* March 1983, p. 15.

36. Dr. Kanter's views summarized in Jean M. Jarvis', "The Innovators: Keys to Successful Organizational and Professional Entrepreneurship," *Hospital Forum,* July/August 1983, p. 38.

37. Ibid.

38. Walter J. McNerney, "Health Care Coalitions," The 1982 Michael M. Davis Lecture presented at The Center for Health Administration Studies, Chicago, 1982. See pp. 11–12 and 17–20.

39. Elliot L. Richardson, "Perspectives on the 'Health Revolution,' " *New England Journal of Medicine* 291, no. 6 (1974), pp. 283–87.

∎4

The providers' symbiotic pursuit of competitive advantage

SURVIVAL OF THE FITTEST—FIT FOR COOPERATION

∎ Hospitals today are being urged to get on the survival curve. They can build successful strategies, Peter Drucker says, for converting turbulence into opportunities if they "take advantage of new realities" and avoid the temptation of denying reality.[1] Howard Berman, an American Hospital Association vice president, has recently noted that some hospitals will ignore these new realities and will not survive. He notes: "The losers will not recognize that the world has changed. Eventually, the world will catch up with them."[2]

The fullest expression of this survival curve theme is in *Can Hospitals Survive?* where Jeff Goldsmith puts the hospital's dilemma into a market concept framework:

> The price of a static definition of organizational or professional purpose in a changing world may be economic failure. In an economic competition, there must be losers as well as winners.[3]

Framing Goldsmith's analysis of the new competitive health care market is his application to the health care field of Alfred Chandler's very powerful notion that American business firms have survived by adapting to changing market pressures.[4] As Goldsmith summarizes:

> According to Chandler's thesis, structural change follows strategic adaptation to the market. Those firms which were unable to adapt failed or were absorbed by their more successful competitors. While one tends to resist using biological metaphors to describe complex human institutions, the similarity between Chandler's thesis to that of biological evolution, Darwin's "survival of the fittest," is rather striking.[5]

Here, Goldsmith identifies the dominant metaphor in the hospital field today—"survival of the fittest." Upon closer inspection, however, his competitive framework contains the underlying survival curve theme that *hospital survival is achieved through the cooperative pursuit of competitive advantage.* He suggests that at this point in their evolution, hospitals are, in Chandler's scheme, midway in the first stage of industrial development—resource accumulation and market control—in which they are "compelled by marketing forces to reexamine their structures and missions as well as their management philosophies."[6] Note that the metaphor of "survival of the fittest" brings with it, as Bennis suggests about all effective metaphors, a compelling necessity for transformation. What, then, must hospitals do? Goldsmith argues that they must develop strategies to confront three "mandates" in today's turbulent times:

1. Horizontal consolidation of hospitals with each other into multihospital systems.
2. Vertical integration of individual and multihospital enterprises and diversification into new lines of health care delivery.
3. Realignment of relationships with the health care professionals without which the system cannot function—physicians and nurses.[7]

Looking at these three mandates, we can see the underlying health care voluntarism theme of cooperation. Goldsmith views the growth of multihospital systems as a trend of "increasing interinstitutional *cooperation.*"[8] His best example of a vertical system (Chicago's Rush-Presbyterian-St. Lukes Medical Center (RPSLMC)) is "a model of *cooperative* and managed multi-institutional relationships which can provide a vehicle for linking health resources together to assure the survival of constituent elements."[9] He stresses hospital-physician joint ventures "if the climate of *cooperation* and interest on the part of physicians exists. Hospitals and physicians should be *allied* in the increasingly competitive health care market, and should strive to maximize their respective advantages."[10] The key in Goldsmith's view to hospitals doing what is necessary is that hospital administrators and physicians accommodate themselves to entrepreneurial managers and physicians in their midsts so that the hospitals can survive in a more competitive world.[11] This is essentially a role-innovator approach. Goldsmith provides the entrepreneurial example of Dr. James Campbell, M.D., CEO of Rush-Presbyterian-St. Lukes Medical Center.[12] This entrepreneurial mentality must be understood, I believe, as being two-sided—a drive towards risk-taking ventures assembled by building consensus and coalitions. Dr. Campbell is not, for example, merely advocating larger share of market here; he is also striving for excellence.

This survival curve message of adaptation through cooperation recently surfaced at a sold-out conference sponsored by the American Hospital Association in cooperation with the American Medical Association. The theme of the conference was "if we—hospitals and physicians—don't hang together, we'll surely hang separately." It was attended by top hospital managers and senior medical staff officers. Meeting planners were surprised by what the *AMA News* reported as "the growing realization among hospital administrators that the survival of their institutions may depend on how much cooperation they can secure from their medical staff."[13] Conference participants felt the dual pressures of regulatory DRG changes in Medicare and increased competition from emerging health care corporations such as HMOs.[14] The bottom line pressure for more cooperation with their hospitals was well understood by physicians at the meeting—hospital survival. As one physician said, "I'm a surgeon. I can't practice without a hospital."[15]

At the conference, physicians debated their possible roles in emerging health care corporations. Dr. David Ottensmeyer, chief executive officer of Albuquerque's Lovelace Health Care Corporation, argues that physicians need to infiltrate the management of emerging health care corporations. He said that integration of physicians into health care corporations "means physicians in top management positions and physicians strategically located throughout the organization at the middle-management level."[16] Dr. Joseph Boyle, chairman of the AMA Board of Trustees, granted the urgency of physicians working closely with hospitals to assure institutional survival, but warned that many physicians are worried about hospitals delivering primary care:

> Hospital administrators can't wait to have their own captive HMO or hospital staff individual practice association over which they can exert much greater control than is possible with an open, independent medical staff.[17]

Competitive forces compelling hospital realignment: market threats and political opportunities

What are the competitive forces driving hospitals to adapt? Michael Porter has suggested that organizations can fail to survive if they define these forces too narrowly, and fail to confront the threats posed by latent sources of competition.[18] He cautions:

> Many managers concentrate so single-mindedly on their direct antagonists in the fight for market share that they fail to realize that they are also competing with their customers and their suppliers for bargaining power. Meanwhile, they also neglect to keep a wary eye out for new entrants to the contest or fail to recognize the subtle threat of substitute products.[19]

Adapting Porter's framework for the purpose of hospital strategic analysis and action, the hospital is confronted by four competitive forces. First, the hospital must compete with existing traditional rivals as well as entering rivals, such as hospital chains. Second, the hospital must confront the danger of service substitutes, such as HMOs. Third, the hospital must bargain with its physicians who may threaten to form hospital substitutes, such as ambulatory surgery centers or shift referrals to a hospital rival. Finally, the hospital must face the awakened payer who may start an HMO or enter into preferred provider organizational contracts that focus its purchasing power.

Porter suggests three action agendas that organizations can adapt in the face of changing competitive forces:

> (1) positioning the company so that its capabilities provide the best defense against the competitive forces; and/or (2) influencing the balance of the forces through strategic moves, thereby improving the company's position; and/or (3) anticipating shifts in the factors underlying the forces and responding to them, with the hope of exploiting change by choosing a strategy appropriate for the new competitive balance before opponents recognize it.[20]

Blue Cross plans and hospitals that sponsored HMOs in the 1970s can be said to have formally or informally adapted an "anticipatory" strategy, having entrepreneurially positioned themselves for the competitive marketplace of the 1980s. Moreover, in forming HMOs, hospitals converted potential threats into alliances—for example, HMO creation by hospitals forged new alliances with physicians and/or payers. In short, each potential competitive threat is also a potential ally in the marketplace. This is one way to convert turbulence into opportunity.

In the 1980s, with insurers emerging as the primary HMO developers, hospitals are likely to adapt the second strategic option—reacting to actual or likely HMO invasion of their market areas which distorts their competitive equilibrium of forces. Faith B. Rafkind, insightfully applying Porter's approach to precisely this situation, suggests the following hospital-HMO scenario and its political ramifications:

> As HMO substitutes enter the geographic service area of a hospital which previously had no major competitive hospital rivals, the balance between that hospital and its key physicians . . . may well shift. The threat of the new entrant, HMO substitute, may forge alliances between hospital trustees, medical staff, and management as they attempt to thwart loss of patients (and market dominance) to the HMO. Thus, the structure of the hospital's environment may be altered.[21]

Thus, the entrance of an HMO into a hospital's environment can trigger a chain reaction that upsets the hospital's traditional balance of competitive pressures and realigns alliances with its physicians and trustees. In a political sense, then, each competitive threat is also an opportunity for alliance building.

THE HOSPITAL'S MARKET: THE SUBSTITUTION SPECTER

A specter haunts the hospital; namely, service substitutes. As Porter suggests, an industry has to be alert for substitute product rivals. This is the lesson being learned today by sugar producers faced with emerging high-fructose corn syrup commercial ventures.[22] A similar danger (and opportunity) of substitute services confronts the hospital. Paul Starr offers the following substitution scenario:

> When the government expanded Medicare and Medicaid, health care became a lucrative investment for the private sector, which responded by investing heavily in hospitals and hospital chains.
>
> With more physicians and more hospitals, lines between the two areas of business are beginning to blur as physicians do more ambulatory surgery and lab work traditionally reserved for hospitals and hospitals set up satellite clinics, taking away some traditional business of the physician.[23]

Goldsmith adds two more hospital substitutes to this picture of the hospital being threatened by physician-sponsored ambulatory care hospital substitutes: alternative delivery systems (ADSs) and aftercare for the elderly.[24] These substitutes overlap and can be substituted for one another. For example, what Goldsmith calls aftercare includes ambulatory care for the elderly, and ADS social-health maintenance organizations (SHMOs) can be developed for the elderly.

HOSPITAL HMO INVOLVEMENT: MOTIVES, ROLES, MISSION, AND EXAMPLE

Motives: From exemplary innovation to vertically-integrated systems

The American Hospital Association has identified eight hospital motives for HMO participation—eight views of HMOs. As a way to:

Learn new lessons in health care delivery.[25]

Offer the consumer options in both the financing and delivery of services.

Obtain a greater share of inpatient admissions.

Obtain a referral network to respond to competition.

Start organized ambulatory care systems.

Establish a new HMO setting for their educational programs.

Win favorable reactions from health systems agencies.

Respond to pressure from organized business or consumers who intend to organize an HMO themselves, unless the hospital takes the lead.[26]

Note that this list begins with the turbulent times notion that hospitals need HMO involvement as an exemplary innovation—one offering important lessons in evolutionary adaptation. Equally important, the list closes with another survival curve point—hospitals, to survive and thrive in an activated environment, must engage in cooperative HMO-like ventures.[27]

Roles: Sponsor, employer, vendor

At the most general level, hospitals have had three types of HMO relationships. The least common was direct *sponsorship* where the hospital's resources were marshaled with the institution at risk. Next, some hospitals acted as *employers* offering their employees the HMO as a health benefit option. Finally, many hospitals became *vendors* to the HMOs selling them inpatient, emergency, and other services. These arrangements were made on a variety of financial terms—fee-for-service, discount, or capitation.[28]

Debate over mission

The traditional debate point against hospital sponsorship of HMOs is that since HMOs reduce hospital utilization, they are in conflict with the hospital's mission. However, in turbulent times, the context of the debate over HMO sponsorship shifts. As Goldsmith argues, to survive in turbulent times, hospitals must be market oriented and must redefine their business. They must see themselves as *health care systems* that reach out to the consumer with options that the customer wants.[29] Moreover, hospitals, as health care systems, will provide services useful to HMOs:

> As the system of health care delivery changes in this country due to declining occupancy rates, cost controls, physician surplus, lack of access to capital, and development of alternative delivery modes, hospitals will be forced to expand and stabilize their own patient bases in order to remain financially viable. One way to accomplish this . . . is to become involved with HMOs.[30]

Dr. James D. Campbell, RPSLMC's president, has an interesting way of using language to lead his organization. He uses a set of aphorisms to communicate his essential messages. In turbulent times, this use of metaphoric language to convey a leader's basic convictions makes eminent sense due to confusion of too much information and mounting uncertainty. Two of his guiding aphorisms help his people convert turbulence into opportunity: "There is safety in numbers," and "Everything has been thought of before; the difficulty is to think of it again."[31] By itself a union demand for better health care benefits is characteristic of turbulent times. Campbell converted it into an opportunity by repackaging the demand as a potential enrollment base for an HMO venture. In doing so, he thought of an innovation "again" in which there was "safety in numbers." In terms of safety in numbers, an HMO is a variation of his voluntaristic vertical integration concept of his institution. As he suggests:

> The case of the idealistic, growing, imperfect Rush vertical system certainly seems to suggest that a "safety in numbers" notion prevails with us for the sake not only of our patients, but also our providers. It seems to offer the plurality and options suggested by competition and yet enables a reasoned cooperation toward rational programs . . .[32]

Blending competition and cooperation, Campbell put the medical center on the survival curve a decade ago.

Medical center example

The Anchor HMO program sponsored by the Rush-Presbyterian-St. Lukes Medical Center (RPSLMC) in Chicago illustrates many of these motives and types of involvement. In terms of roles, Anchor was started as an alternative benefit for medical center workers. It was solely sponsored by the medical center which continues to deliver most of the HMO's hospital and ancillary services.[33] In terms of motivation, the immediate trigger was a hospital worker union demand for a health benefit option that would increase availability, affordability, and comprehensiveness of coverage. This demand took place in the context of medical center leadership's emerging strategic plan to convert the hospital into a collaborative, vertical system that included primary-care satellites to act as patient feeders into the medical center, in addition to a medical school that could use an HMO for teaching and training purposes.

Figures 4–1, 4–2, and 4–3 analyze the advantages and disadvantages of HMO sponsorship.

FIGURE 4–1 ■ Advantages to the medical center of HMO sponsorship

---

The advantages to RPSLMC of sponsoring an HMO are evident in some areas and not so evident in others. These advantages include the following:

1. *The HMO increases inpatient utilization.*

   To the extent that an HMO attracts members that otherwise would not be hospitalized at the sponsoring institution, the institution could benefit from increased inpatient utilization. In this sense, institutions that are experiencing low utilization could look towards an HMO as a means of increasing utilization. In 1981, Anchor was responsible for providing 20,000 total patient days of care, of which 11,500 were at RPSLMC.

2. *The HMO can utilize the hospital's ancillary/administrative services.*

   By spreading the direct and indirect costs of providing ancillary services over a large base volume, the unit costs of providing the service can be reduced through economies of scale. Because Anchor purchases a large volume of ancillary services from Rush, the medical center may benefit from inherent economies of scale and consequently be more cost effective per unit of service provided. This may result in lowering health care costs and/or decreasing the rate of increase in these costs.

3. *The HMO allows the hospital to establish linkages with community hospitals.*

   The HMO establishes relationships with community hospitals for hospitalization, referrals, emergency services, and so forth. These relationships could be with hospitals that may or may not have been affiliated with the medical center. In either case, these referral patterns and affiliations can form the

(Fig. 4–1 Cont.)

basis for further relationships which may be mutually beneficial. For example, in the case of RPSLMC, the following advantages could accrue:

a. The medical center may rotate their residents and interns in community hospitals.

b. The medical center specialists may serve as consultants to the medical staff of the community hospital.

c. The medical center may get most of the referrals for tertiary care from the nonHMO physicians.

d. The medical center may provide a combination of administrative/financial/computer/shared services support for the community hospital and may therefore achieve some economies of scale.

4. *HMO physicians can be involved in teaching and research.*

All staff physicians at Anchor have a faculty appointment at the medical center and devote a minimum of four hours per week to academic pursuits. Several members of Anchor's physician staff have held or hold senior faculty appointments such as Director of the OB/GYN residency program, Associate Professor of the Department of Preventive Medicine and Director of Pediatric Clerkships. Thus, it appears evident that the medical center stands to benefit from the additional academic involvement and support from the HMO physicians.

5. *The HMO exposes residents/interns to an alternative delivery system.*

Source: "Private Sector Investment in HMOs: A Case Study of Hospital Sponsorship," (Rockville, Md.: Department of Health and Human Services, 1982), pp. 8–9.

FIGURE 4–2 ■ Disadvantages to the medical center of HMO sponsorship

The main hurdle faced by the medical center when the decision to sponsor the HMO was being contemplated was the element of "risk." The development of a staff model HMO required capital and human resource outlays as risk capital which could be lost if the HMO was a failure. It took approximately 10 years of cautious expansion and operation before Anchor's revenues exceeded its expenses. Therefore, the sponsoring institution must not only be prepared to make a substantial investment, but it must be willing to wait a long time before it sees any tangible returns on that investment. Thus, the institution must have a corporate strategy of long-range growth.

Another area to consider is the possibility of physician reluctance to participate in prepaid delivery systems. In the case of Rush, this did not appear to be a problem. The academic nature and diversity of practice modalities at the medical center coupled with the skillful manner in which the HMO was presented to the medical staff helped to diffuse potential resistance.

Source: "Private Sector Investment in HMOs: A Case Study of Hospital Sponsorship," (Rockville, Md.: Department of Health and Human Services, 1982), pp. 9–10.

FIGURE 4–3 ■ Advantages/disadvantages to Anchor of medical center sponsorship

---

In order for a relationship between two parties to be successful, it must provide mutual benefits. The success of Anchor must be partially attributed to the fact that it was sponsored by a large prestigious medical center that was willing to support it with financial and human resources. Needless to say, Anchor has derived several benefits from hospital sponsorship and, even though they will not be discussed in detail, a delineation is provided below:

Enabled Anchor to start up quickly.

Provided a source of interest-free loans to cover start-up costs and any operating deficits.

Enabled Anchor to obtain a competitive fringe benefit package.

Helped Anchor to more readily attract staff physicians because of the prestige of the association with a major medical center.

Provided a vast array of subspecialists that could handle all referrals from Anchor.

Enhanced Anchor's marketing efforts with the medical center's affiliation.

Provided financial and diagnostic services at competitive rates to Anchor.

Enabled Anchor to operate under a philosophy of long-range development.

Some of the disadvantages to Anchor of medical center sponsorship include:

Most of Anchor's hospitalization is done at Rush where the cost of a hospital day is expensive compared to a community hospital.

Anchor has not been able to advertise its programs as strongly as it would like because of the "conservative" nature of the medical center and its staff.

In the short range Anchor's contractual arrangements for radiology, financial services, and so on, were advantageous, but they may not prove to be so in the long run when the cost of buying their services remains competitive. In other words, Anchor could become "locked in" to contractual arrangements that may not be competitive.

Because Anchor is a component of the medical center, its long-range planning and development has to take place within the context of the corporate long-range strategy. While this may be advantageous in one sense, it also places some constraints in the planning and expansion of Anchor.

Source: "Private Sector Investment in HMOs: A Case Study of Hospital Sponsorship," (Rockville, Md.: Department of Health and Human Services, 1982), p. 10–11.

HOSPITAL HMO INVOLVEMENT AMID SHIFTING COMPETITIVE PRESSURES

The Group Health Association of America (GHAA) has recently analyzed the results of the 1982 national HMO census. They call attention to the pattern of HMO sponsorship to date. GHAA notes that hospitals were involved in sponsoring 44 new HMOs and have been the fourth most frequent HMO developer since 1970. GHAA suggests that in the 1970s, hospitals sponsored HMOs as competitive responses to other HMOs entering their markets. GHAA goes on to add that since 74 percent of the areas with HMOs as yet have had no hospital HMO development response, it is reasonable to assume that hospitals in these markets constitute a new set of HMO sponsors.[34] Moreover, with increased HMO venturing by insurers and other HMO investors, hospitals and insurers will be seeking each other out in the 1980s to explore joint ventures.

HOSPITAL INNOVATION: PHYSICIAN CULTURE AND SYMBIOTIC MANAGEMENT

Organizational development and physician culture

The professional core of health care institutions—the hospital's doctors—produces unique resistance to change, joint ventures, and so on. Innovative efforts to improve medical center productivity through the application of organizational development (OD) techniques reveal this physician resistance. For the most part, these efforts have failed.[35] Those who have tried to establish innovative health care programs through the use of OD techniques have called attention to the difference between the health care field and other industries. In industrial organizations, the structure is hierarchical, the product is well defined, and management is in control. In contrast, in health care institutions, the structure is collegial, the product diffuse and varied (patient care, research, and teaching), and control is shared with governing bodies and physicians.[36]

Innovative efforts in health care organizations must carefully consider physician culture. This traditional physician culture has been characterized as follows:

> The physician is bred and trained to take charge in his workshop. The expectation of authority is the key element in the physician's perspective . . . we argue specifically that the dominant perspective of physicians includes two elements: acceptance of ultimate responsibility for the health of the *individual* patient for whom responsibility is accepted; and the related right to control the workplace in the interest of insuring professional autonomy.[37]

To a significant extent, the traditional practice of medicine tends to pursue autonomous goals in relation to other systems in its environment (e.g., administrative and governance), and faces the potential hazards of such autonomous goals. Autonomous goals and their hazards have been defined as those which:

> assume that the system or organism is completely independent of all others; it is completely self-governing. Such goals inevitably lead to overspecialization,

compartmentalization, or empire building and bureaucracy—to duplication, stasis, and inevitable death . . . For autonomous systems, there is no feedback from the environment—none is desired.[38]

There is, then, a tendency for autonomy—voluntary action not guided by external checks and balances—to adopt a power-over stance. Leaders who have attempted OD techniques in medical centers explain their lack of success by noting that their approach only reinforces what health care institutions already have—physician autonomy. In these situations, autonomous goals have been identified as the main problem to overcome: overspecialization, duplication, and fragmentation of services as well as poor coordination between professional, management, and governance systems. Leaders, therefore, recommend increased degrees of coordination and organization in health care institutions.[39]

Increased organization within traditional institutions (and increased competition between traditional and alternative delivery systems), however, runs counter to the traditional physician culture and its autonomy imperative. The traditional culture—with considerable justification—sees such organizational and competitive goals as potential hazards to the personal physician-patient relationship. The traditional view holds that the solo form of practice and the payment of fees for each service to the practitioner are necessary to preserve this one-to-one relationship. But are all organizational and competitive goals necessarily antagonistic to this relationship? Prepaid group practice leaders think not. They suggest that the two kinds of goals can complement one another.

Symbiotic management

In prepaid group practice, physicians are integrated into management in a way analogous to what Peter Drucker has suggested for all professionals in organizations. He urges that professionals be integrated into an organization's financial planning and administrative processes so that they come to understand what management is up against in making business decisions. He suggests that:

> the professional who has had to think through his own objective and appraise his own performance and contribution against goals he has himself set, soon comes to understand what decision making involves and what "performance" really means. He does not cease to be a "professional"; he must not cease to be one. But he acquires an additional dimension of understanding, additional vision, and the sense of responsibility for the survival and performance of the whole that distinguishes the manager from the subordinate and the citizen from the subject.[40]

This amounts to a shift in professional and organizational cultures.

Over the years, proponents of prepaid group practice have sought to define how their organizational culture differs from that of traditional medical care. The term *health maintenance organization* suggests part of this difference—prepaid group practices are more *organized* than the traditional practice and view this organization as complementary to good medical practice. Cecil Cutting, M.D., of the Kaiser-Permanente program, has labeled the medical group-health plan relationship a process of "symbiotic management." He notes that physicians are responsible for making this symbiosis work: "It is the physicians' acceptance of responsibility for providing comprehensive care to the membership, and his responsible role as a partner in administrating the program, that are the keys to unlocking the potential of a rational organization of medical care."[41] This symbiotic value means that physicians overtly recognize that the practice of medicine happens in an increasingly organized world—one where resources are limited and in need of efficient management. Thus, whereas traditional physicians are prone to view many forms of increased organization—including prepaid group practice—as antagonistic to their professional autonomy, prepaid physicians tend to see increased organization and responsibility for a defined population of members—*within limits*—as beneficial to their goals. Kaiser physicians are integrated in the HMO's management, as Drucker suggests.

One aspect of industry that closely approximates this symbiotic health care situation is technological innovation. It helps clarify the power-with approach to organizations. Bell Telephone Labs., Inc., like the management of Kaiser-Permanente, uses the term *symbiosis* to describe its management-professional culture: "The professionals must feel a personal symbiosis with the whole process, as well as with their professional world."[42] Bell Labs' management sees symbiotic goals as those which "recognize that any system is always a part of a larger system containing other similar and different species. Symbiotic goals encourage a mutually beneficial living together with all other symbionts. They recognize that complementary benefits and mutual help are necessary from all species for maximum survival."[43] Management then views itself not as autonomously over or antagonistically against the professionals, but as symbiotically with them in the service of a common purpose. This is essentially a power-with stance. Survival and success are sought through symbiosis.

The symbiotic culture at Bell Labs has six additional characteristics or beliefs. The first two are shared by the traditional physician culture—all six are shared by prepaid group practices. The characteristics are:

The key resource is *professionals.* Their satisfaction is a key factor.

The professional *viewpoint* and autonomy is a vital ingredient.

Management recognizes the prime role of professionals and provides them with *opportunities* (e.g., all organization, equipment, facilities, and so on.) to practice.

Management helps coordinate professionals with various specialties into *groups* to attack comprehensive problems.

The only *limitation* on professional autonomy and managerial conduct is that both must serve the overall organization's mission: "To provide the best communications service at the lowest price consistent with financial health." (Change "best" to "most satisfactory and accessible," "communication" to "health," and we get an excellent prepaid group practice plan corporate purpose.)

The overall organization has a social responsibility.[44]

Recent events have made Bell Labs' health care analogy even more interesting—"the phone company" no longer enjoys monopoly status. It now finds itself in a turbulent marketplace. In the face of this new reality, Ma Bell's key R&D workers—the counterpart to health care's physicians—are now being examined in the new light of cost control. *Fortune* observes:

> As Ma Bell's prodigy for nearly six decades, Bell Telephone Laboratories was doted on for bravura performances at the frontiers of research . . . In the wealthy Bell family, the Labs got special attention often accorded a prodigy—clout in family councils, a big allowance. But, as the family disbands, this favored offspring faces a loss of indulgence.[45]

As the traditional health care field becomes more competitive, there will be an increasing need to adapt its familylike voluntary culture to new marketplace realities. The symbiosis metaphor offers a path for balancing cooperation and competition in turbulent times.

Symbiotic management's four levels

Prepaid group practices show this symbiotic format at four levels of organization: a defined population that becomes the basis of its corporate mission, the stress on group practice, the medical group-health plan relationship, and a stress on competition. By elaborating on these levels, we find that prepaid group practices enlarge the traditional physician value system to include responsibility not only for the individual patient, but also for the program's defined population of members.

Population. One prepaid group practice medical director, Phillip Chu, M.D., has noted that in a group practice setting, success of the group is viewed in terms of the entire group's culture. He continues:

> Most important, we encounter serious difficulty in starting a prepaid program when the group cannot adopt a new concept in medicine which does not exist in fee-for-service medical practice; that is, the sense of responsibility of the medical group for the protection of the health of the enrolled membership. This is quite a different responsibility from that of the physician who does a good technical job with the individual patient who chooses to walk into his office.[46]

Medical group. The alternative practice program stresses that physicians be organized into formal medical groups. Chu describes the stress of formal physician organization (note his preoccupation with the problem of *implementing* such a collaborative organization):

> [I]n group practice . . . the major task still remains to be tackled—*how to organize and motivate* the group. How do you get the group to function together for the common objective? How to remunerate the group so it is not divisive? How do you organize the functions of the clinic and staff so that they work together as a team?[47]

Health plan. Prepaid group practices typically consist of two *organizations: (a)* an insurance-like health plan that sells health policies and is thereby responsible to its subscribers for arranging that all covered services be provided and *(b)* a medical delivery system that actually provides the services. As a *closed system* (characterized by an annually enrolled population of subscribers and income from subscribers' fees, benefits, and so on), these two organizations must live within set budgets and hence have direct incentives to work together.[48]

Competitive goals. The traditional physician perspective views competition as antagonistic—tending towards predatory power-over practices and a diluting of the product. The Kaiser-Permanente organization and other prepaid programs believe that market competition between alternative and traditional consumer options adds a healthy dose of free enterprise into a "quasi-monopolistic tradition" of fee-for-service medicine.[49] The idea here is that such competition is good; that is, symbiotic for both options.

HOSPITAL INNOVATION DECISION MAKING AS NEGOTIATION AND CONFLICT RESOLUTION

The hospital administrator as innovation champion

Those who have tried organizational development techniques to innovate in medical centers suggest that increased institutional organization and coordination can be accomplished by pilot projects directed by people who show a "sensitivity to political and interpersonal processes."[50] This, of course, is the role-innovator approach. The administrators of a hospital who choose to experiment with more symbiotic relationships with physicians must, like their insurance company and business/labor role innovator counterparts, do four things:

Advocate innovation and provide strong, continued leadership.

Gain a technical comprehension of the innovation.

Harness external pressure to serve their innovation mission.

Act sensitively to the political process of their organization.

These four aspects of hospital role innovating are illustrated in the experience of the administrators of the Long Island–Jewish Medical Center (LIJ).[51] The first three are similar to those exhibited by innovative insurers. Administrators at LIJ showed considerable commitment and staying power in their innovation championing in the face of substantial resistance. One administrator had years of prepaid group practice experience and was a recognized authority on the alternative. The medical center's administrator fully used local Blue Cross interest in starting a prepaid group practice to move his own organization into action. Again, like their insurance company counterparts, hospital role innovators were skilled in their organization's political process. Since hospitals differ from insurance company bureaucracies, this section will focus on the political conflict resolution aspect of hospital innovating.

The prepaid group practice concept is typically seen by a hospital medical staff as running counter to their sense of physician identity. This produces resistance to and disagreements about the innovation. Administrators must gain the assent of the hospital's board for prepaid group practice development while keeping medical staff resistance at some workable level. How is this done?

Decision-making model

Some researchers who have studied the problems of physician identity within hospitals that have innovated see the decision-making process as essentially one of negotiation and conflict resolution. They have identified four negotiation strategies used to resolve conflict and disagreement: problem solving, persuasion, bargaining, and political negotiation. They describe these as follows:

> In problem solving, one must assume that objectives are shared . . . The use of persuasion assumes the belief that at some point ultimate objectives are shared and disagreement over subgoals is mediated by reference to ultimately shared objectives . . . Where bargaining is used, disagreement without persuasion is sought . . . In the game of political negotiation, the arena of bargaining is not taken as fixed by the participants and allegiances with third parties are frequently sought.[52]

For our purposes, it is useful to convert these static approaches into a four-step negotiation process. In step one, administrators adopt a problem-solving approach both to technically explore the prepaid group concept and to educate the medical staff. This sets the stage for the next three strategies—persuasion, bargaining, and political negotiation. The first two stages (problem solving and persuasion) are power-with steps built on or working toward a common goal. The last two steps (bargaining and political negotiating) are power-over steps lacking basic agreement. This four-step model of a political decision-making process with its power-over steps portrays typical medical center innovating where there is major resistance to change.

LIJ's lay, professional, and administrative leadership had long recognized a basic "failure to deliver continuous, comprehensive care on an ambulatory basis." Problem identification, however, did not lead to change. Proposed change was resisted. The medical center's administrative leaders ran into three obstacles: *(a)* the LIJ's teaching mission had to be protected and enhanced by any change, *(b)* the attending medical staff believed that fee-for-service practitioners out in the community were adequately providing ambulatory care, and *(c)* there was no financial incentive for the medical center to begin to provide ambulatory care. This impasse was broken when the local Blue Cross Plan suggested to the medical center staff the possibility of a partnership to develop a prepaid group practice. LIJ's administrative leadership, including a physician with substantial prepaid group practice experience, saw the proposal as a way to act on the medical center's ambulatory care problem in an organized fashion. They championed the PGP proposal.

The medical center adopted a *problem-solving* approach by forming a task force to examine the feasibility of starting a prepaid group practice in partnership with the Blue Cross Plan. The task force concluded that the venture was technically feasible and desirable. Recognizing that the venture also had to be acceptable to the center's medical staff, the administrators turned their attention to seeking internal support. They were able to *persuade* the departmental chairmen that the proposed program was not antagonistic to their own beliefs—they were institution based and on salary themselves—and that it would not harm but enhance the teaching program. The result was that the chairmen supported the administration in its prepaid group practice proposal to the LIJ board.

However, the voluntary medical staff's reaction was even more antagonistic than expected. The administrators had anticipated a hostile reaction to the proposal since it challenged the traditional physician culture, and had adopted a *bargaining* posture with built-in safeguards—the project would be experimental and on a limited scale. But these safeguards were inadequate to allay the voluntary staff's fears of being confronted with a competitive medical alternative. They felt the administration was acting in bad faith by proposing what amounted to a threat to the very physicians that had helped the center achieve its excellent reputation. Educational meetings and persuasive efforts failed. The staff *politicized* the situation by going outside the bargaining room and using personal contracts to influence the board.

The administration countered by bringing in third parties, such as noted health care authorities, to legitimate the proposal. A crucial third party— the president of the Blue Cross Plan—personally appealed to the board to support the venture. Equally important, the Blue Cross Plan agreed to take on much of the financial risk of the venture. In short, the Blue Cross CEO was the innovation patron. His offer enabled the board to think less in terms of risk and more in terms of opportunity. Despite medical staff opposition, the board gave its approval to conduct a pilot prepaid group practice program. The administration had successfully *negotiated* a decision to proceed with innovation development.

Variations on a theme

Edward Connors has identified three obstacles to diversification into primary care.[53] First, hospital trustees need to have a clear concept of the hospital's mission as something more than providing inpatient services. Second, it must be understood that there may be medical staff opposition that must be addressed openly and should not be permitted to block hospital decision making and action. Third, the financial dimension cannot be ignored. The LIJ HMO story reveals strong administrative leadership but an unclear picture of corporate mission and firmness in facing medical staff opposition.

It is, therefore, instructive to compare the LIJ venture with other hospital-sponsored HMO efforts. An excellent example—one showcased by the American Hospital Association—of a hospital enlarging its business definition is Cincinnati's Good Samaritan Hospital (GSH). GSH has reconceptualized itself as a health care corporation offering access to a comprehensive set of services, and has taken on the responsibility of enhancing its community's health.[54] Cosponsoring an HMO was one way to act as a health care corporation. Operationally, its HMO involvement meant the overt recognition of its ambulatory care services as a distinct product line. Moreover, GSH's president involved the medical staff early in the planning process, and when the medical staff failed to endorse the board's decision to cosponsor an HMO with Blue Cross, she implemented the board's decision to establish a medical group to staff the HMO.[55]

The HMO story in Detroit presents some further variations of the hospital HMO sponsorship theme. Ford Motor Company, concerned about mounting health care costs, provided the impetus for HMO development in Detroit.[56] Like the AFL–CIO in Cincinnati, Ford brought in Kaiser-Permanente consultants to do an expert feasibility study. Their judgment was that a locally developed, quality group practice model would work reasonably well in the Detroit area to serve blue-collar clients.

Unlike the situation in Cincinnati, Kaiser expressed no interest in being the Detroit HMO developer. Ford turned to Ford Hospital as the essential coalition builder. Decision making was simply structured—the Ford family was represented on both auto and hospital boards. Moreover, Ford Hospital was a high-quality provider with a long-standing commitment to primary care. Its management accepted a mandate to implement the Kaiser recommendations.[57] This was carved out as part of a formal effort of reconceptualizing the hospital in the aftermath of the tumultuous 1960s and the emerging competitive market of the 1980s. Somewhat like GSH, Ford Hospital proceeded despite considerable medical staff misgivings. As Dr. Bruce Steinhauer recently observed:

> If it was put to a vote by our physician staff, we don't put things to a vote at Ford Hospital, but, if we had done so, it probably would not have passed. As a collegial decision, however, we did ultimately decide that we should get at this. The compelling argument for doing so, we felt, was that it would help defend and expand our market share.[58]

Dr. Steinhauer also made two other innovative evaluation points. First, he noted that HMOs feature the kind of discipline on utilization that hospitals will need anyway in a world of DRGs (diagnosis related groups); that is, HMOs provide some useful organizational change lessons. Second, he noted that many community hospitals lack Ford's enormous resources and integration of administration and medical staff. This leads him to conclude: "The political implications of introducing to a community hospital anything other than an IPA [individual practice association] are difficult, especially now."[59] We turn to IPA development next.

ENTREPRENEURIAL CHAMPIONING OF AN IPA: LEARNING ABOUT RISK TAKING BY OBTAINING AGREEMENTS

In 1980, a community hospital-Blue Cross Plan IPA joint venture was launched in the Boston area. How this came about illustrates many of the basic power-with principles of survival curve management for the turbulent 1980s. In this section I will review this venture in terms of these basic principles.[60]

An innovation champion emerges to "think consensus"

The hospital's vice president of financial affairs went to an HMO conference in 1972. He became committed to the concept and called it to the attention of the hospital's president.[61] The vice president was well respected inside the hospital for his technical skills which were recognized as being vital to the organization's survival. He also had excellent relationships with insurer counterparts outside the organization. In 1976, he was informally assigned as HMO champion.[62] He viewed the championing task as essentially a consensus-building challenge. He recalls:

> When I was trying to get the HMO going, I didn't think about [abstract concepts like] marketing. I was thinking about how to get the divergent interests [physicians, trustees, hospital administration and insurance company management] working together—establishing a forum for trust, credibility, and all those things to happen.[63]

The innovation patron acts to create security for innovators

The president bided his time until 1976 when his contract was up for renewal. At this juncture, he discussed renewal with the chairman of the hospital's board in the context of the management challenge facing the institution. Essentially, he argued that turbulent times required that the hospital's administrators feel secure in promoting risky innovations, such as HMOs. Influential in his decision to sign on for eight more years was the trustees accepting his patronage of such innovators. He got this mandate for change and picked the financial vice president to champion the HMO concept, stressing his practical as opposed to ideological approach to problem solving.[64] Once he decided to proceed with the HMO initiative, he argued publicly to the board and medical staff that the HMO was good for all concerned, and he privately caucused with the key trustee and medical leadership to identify problems and seek constructive solutions.[65]

Exemplary innovation for turbulent times

Beyond the very powerful motive of protecting market share, the innovation champion saw HMO involvement as a "low-risk training ground for broader organizational change efforts."[66] He saw the health care field as undergoing rapid transformation featuring cost containment, risk taking, vertical integration diversification, and capitation payments for services. Moreover, he saw the necessity for swift, adaptive action by the hospital for it to survive.[67] HMO involvement was, in his view, a way to get the hospital's management, physician, and trustee constituencies moving into and thinking about these new realities.

Impetus

The spark that ignited real movement on HMO involvement was an approach in 1977 by a nearby university-sponsored prepaid group practice HMO. This HMO explored the possibility of affiliation with the hospital. The hospital's medical staff was opposed. Nonetheless, the HMO's approach brought with it the real possibility of entering the hospital's market territory one way or another. Something had to be done to protect the hospital's market share against possible HMO invasion.[68]

Sorting out alternatives: Internal negotiations and external alliance building

Key medical staff physicians persuaded key trustees to reject the HMO's offer of alliance. In exchange, the physicians agreed to explore other HMO operations. Management discussed the situation with members of the medical staff and persuaded them that something needed to be done about the threat of HMOs entering the hospital's market. In turn, the managers recognized that successful HMO implementation required medical staff support in planning.[69] A board subcommittee was established, and it selected the IPA approach as most compatible with the hospital's culture. Moreover, it recommended a joint venture with an insurer who was known to be interested in HMOs. The insurer could bring to the alliance several important ingredients for success:

1. Risk capital.
2. HMO development experience.
3. Reputable marketing capacity.
4. Not-for-profit status.
5. Good community image.[70]

Moreover, the hospital already had a good working relationship with the insurer's HMO patron and HMO champion. The insurer saw, in its proposed HMO alliance with the hospital, a vital building block in its emerging strategy of cost containment—in the words of an involved HMO manager, through a marriage between hospitals and insurers. "Control efforts won't suffice. Being able to develop cooperative hospital-insurer interfaces is probably the most important thing to the Blue Cross Plan."[71]

Structuring the decision field to build an innovation enclave

The planning process was structured to build a consensus among HMO proponents necessary for implementation. "Medical staff members participated as individuals—not as formal representatives of the hospital medical staff . . . Assembling a small nucleus of primary care physicians was the crucial determinant of HMO development."[72] This gave the managers a subset of physicians with whom to cooperatively plan an IPA. They became a pro-HMO physician constituency within the medical staff. Moreover, these physicians were realistic negotiators willing to sit down, discuss the issues, and explore perspectives that were different from their own. Further, as hard-headed negotiators, these physicians bargained for reassurances concerning their economic stake in any venture.

The deciding as debate, caucus, and negotiation

The hospital's internal decision-making process on the HMO venture was marked by "participant willingness to open themselves up to conflict and manage conflict through a cumbersome and time-consuming process of open debate, negotiation, and operation of a consensus decision rule."[73] For example, trustee HMO proponents would openly debate anti-HMO physicians on explosive issues. This signaled to the medical staff the depth of the board's support of management's initiative which in turn helped provide interested physicians with the confidence necessary to engage in HMO discussion.[74]

Crucial to the success of public debate was private caucusing between patron, champion, and key physician and trustee leaders on how the medical staff and board would see issues as they arose and who on the staff and board might move into the pro-HMO enclave. This did two things: First, it allowed the pro-HMO debaters to make their best case and second, it helped build the essential core of interested physicians.[75] As a process of public debate and private caucusing, strategy formulation was highly informal. Policy "positions" were not adopted going into the discussion, but emerged from the give-and-take negotiation issues as they came up.[76]

A cooperative outlook: Joint hospital-physician-insurer decision making

In 1978, an informal, nine-member work group composed of three representatives each from the insurance company, the hospital, and the physician staff was established. This group was formally recognized in early 1979. It was this body that got HMO decisions processed by hard-headed negotiations which resolved issues and the conflict they raised.[77] A key issue was sponsorship. Physicians at first were for a hospital-sponsored HMO. The insurer, however, was the party that was bringing the venture capital to the table, and it wanted to be the HMO sponsor. The physicians examined their position and found their essential interest: they sought sponsor status in order to avoid being controlled by the insurer or the HMO. On examining the power-with realities of HMO operation, the physicians saw that the HMO would legally be merely an insurer product line, but in practice had to operate as a joint venture with the hospital and its physicians. If the insurer acted in any arbitrary fashion, the physicians could withdraw, and the HMO would fail. Operationalizing this cooperative outlook, HMO decisions would be made by a power-with joint management committee (JMC) with one third of its members being physicians.[78] As the insurer's HMO champion observes:

> Ultimately, all parties had to work together, based on trust and structural counterbalances provided by the JMC. Everyone was paranoid about turf, but knew that if the venture were to succeed, no one corporation could dominate.[79]

In conclusion, competitive survival requires continuing cooperation.

IMPLEMENTATION OF A PREPAID GROUP PRACTICE

Physician leadership is key to building organizational culture

A review of our argument so far reveals an implementation dilemma. Medical centers/hospitals seek to innovate in prepaid-group-practice-like ways, but such innovations run into medical staff opposition. Administrators can overpower this resistance by heavy-handed political means. The dilemma is that management cannot create a new medical system by the same political or administrative means. Medical organization and mutuality are not achieved by power-over fiat. This problem is the counterpart to the one we discussed concerning the Rochester situation where purchaser fiat was not sufficient to assure proper marketing of the new prepaid group practice. Prepaid medical group principles, such as symbiotic management, are not self-propelled; they must be effectively converted into action. As one expert has concluded:

> To attempt to visualize the structure of a medical group in advance of the actual operation is essential, but it will not create a functioning organization. The manner in which implementation takes place may so divert the program from the course intended by its planners that it can never be restored to their original purpose.[80]

Implementation, then, is a crucial step.

This point is a direct conclusion from the experience of the prepaid group practice movement. In 1958, the Kaiser-Permanente management and board, for example, made a decision to develop a prepaid group practice program in Hawaii. They built a $4 million hospital, recruited a medical staff, and opened the doors. After several years it was clear that the effort was a failure and had to be started again with a new medical group.[81] One Kaiser medical leader concluded that the initial venture failed because management had ignored its own principles acquired in over 15 years of successful prepaid group programs developed on the West Coast. Members of the original medical group had not developed a commitment to the prepaid principle of physician responsibility—there had been no physician leader to instill such a loyalty.[82] Kaiser-Permanente had not recreated its organizational culture in Hawaii.

The medical director's role in cultivating symbiosis

The physician leader is the program's medical director. His job is to develop a cohesive medical group and to maintain a symbiotic relationship with the program's management and clientele. As Dr. Conrad Rosenberg, a prepaid group practice medical director, puts it:

> The symbiotic relationship . . . requires that physicians and all staff assume the role of more than just a provider of care. Each must assist in the success of the program by being sensitive to its administrative problems and its unique characteristic as opposed to the somewhat isolated and nonaccountable experiences of fee-for-service practice. Symbiotic management involves an awareness that periodically adversary roles may be appropriate during a period of negotiation, but, that when this process is finished, the roles cannot be perpetuated.[83]

As a role innovator, the medical director works skillfully at the interface between his organization and the plan—interpreting, translating, distilling views and values, and negotiating interest. He maximizes the interests of his group by keeping it well organized—within the context of the health of the overall medical group-health plan relationship and program. This is an exercise in power-with political skills.

According to Dr. Robert Match of the Long Island–Jewish Medical Center, the prepaid group practice medical director does the following:

1. He must set a professional example for his fellow physicians in their standards of practice.
2. He requires a deep understanding of the economic complexities of providing quality care at predetermined cost; this, of course, implies a complete dedication to the principles of full-time practice and income pooling.
3. He must have the confidence and understanding of whatever governing board has responsibility for the creation and marketing of the health plan.
4. He must provide a leadership example to all nonmedical personnel who are an integral part of the care delivery unit.
5. He is often the determinant in how effectively the internal mechanics of group operation meet the needs of the patients.
6. He must function at all times as the advocate of the subscriber in gaining access to the system in a timely and meaningful way.
7. He is the key to the opening of lines of communication between the physician and the representatives of the consumers. Conversely, he must design methods of insulating the physicians from unreasonable and unrealistic demands from the patient population.
8. He must have an in-depth knowledge and concern about the economic health of the plan. This means monitoring and influencing utilization, and so on; conveying this knowledge to his fellow physicians in intelligible fashion; and engender in them a cooperative understanding of the importance of these factors to their own economic future.
9. He must be able to cope with a variety of external organizations with which the group must deal—often in a hostile environment. These may include local medical societies, hospital medical boards, and so on.[84]

Clearly, such an interdisciplinary set of tasks requires considerable sensitivity to political and group processes. Dr. Rosenberg remarks that the prepaid group practice medical director must be skillful in the exercise of power as well as

> somewhat aggressive, competitive, and enjoy exercising control . . . Add on a faculty for masking or channeling these unlovely attributes, and coupling them with a sense of proportion and timing in assessing those issues which merit expression, and those which are unimportant and do not . . . Lastly,

there is the ability to experience a very personal pleasure in giving a little bit more than one is taking from the endeavor. The "little bit" is rather important, for one who derives enormous pleasure in giving and very little in receiving often expects the same from colleagues, which is unreal.[85]

An example of where such symbiotic leadership is needed is in the central planning task of annual medical group budget preparation. This task must be integrated with the larger one of preparing the HMO program's overall budget which also includes administrative and inpatient components. Since these components interact, strong medical leadership and participation in the plan's budget is called for. Dr. Ernest Saward observes:

> The medical group as a whole almost always wishes to be overprotective of itself in planning such budgets, a veritable doomsday view with contingency for all the possible adverse factors at once. Quite obviously, the dues structure is subject to the discipline of the market place and negotiated benefits. Suffice it to say, the medical director will be the leader in realistically untangling the skein.[86]

Moreover, Saward notes that this budget necessitates, over the course of the year, a self-discipline by the medical group of how they use up resources. Only through continuous and strong medical director leadership does the group come to be aware of and accept such discipline.[87]

A participatory approach to medical director recruitment and training

Finding physician leaders is difficult. The prepaid medical group director's job description calls for a near superman, and the supply of seasoned supermen is limited. One common and practical approach is to use the program planning period as an aid to recruitment. This has three advantages: First, participation in planning provides opportunities for local physicians to become involved in the program on an advisory basis, which allows them to test their interest in prepaid group practice. Often, one of these advisors decides to play a leadership role. As one medical director recalls about the planning process: "Soon I realized that a medical director was needed and that I'd be pretty jealous of the guy that got chosen."[88] He decided to apply for the job himself. Second, early input by the program's prospective leader allows him to make important contributions and informal judgments of its soundness and prospects for success. A physician leader with the Kaiser program notes that:

> To have the proper attitude, enthusiasm, and identification, the medical director should be in on the planning phase. I would not accept the tremendous responsibilities . . . unless I was given early opportunity for input into the development of the system to be operated. . . . The planning and development of a new, prepaid group practice, without physician input, greatly increases the chance of performance failure in the eyes of any potential medical director.[89]

Third, the planning process serves as an excellent means of developing the physician leader for his medical director role.

Forming the medical group

Next, the physician leader must attract and organize interested physicians into a cohesive prepaid group practice team. This process involves two dilemmas: How to recruit physicians to an organization that does not yet exist, and how recruited physicians who are new to "strange" prepaid group practice principles and used to the traditional perspective can give the alternative a fair test. A variety of solutions to these problems have been tried. The effort of a leading multispecialty medical group, the Marshfield (Wisconsin) Clinic, in becoming involved in prepaid practice illustrates one solution. In the early 1970s, the clinic undertook prepaid development as a joint venture and an experiment with the local Blue Cross Plan. The Blue Cross Plan would be the HMO plan, and the clinic would provide the program's medical services. The clinic made a partial conversion to prepayment—its physicians agreed to see some patients on a prepaid group practice basis. The first problem was solved by using existing staff. The second problem was solved by trial and error. Reflecting on the lessons learned by the clinic in launching the HMO, the clinic's president identified several caveats, two of which are:

> Make sure the medical staff understands completely what your HMO plan provides. Our apparent failure to do so is one of the reasons we lost money . . . Add staffing specifically for primary care. We thought we wouldn't have to . . . It's proven a difficult adjustment. Recently, we did create a primary department so we're finally staffed to provide primary care. Yet, we're finding this an area of continuing consternation.[90]

We can see here that simple adaptation of existing resources and procedures to the new prepaid scheme proved insufficient. Another solution to the medical group organizing problem is the "sole-proprietor" approach which is illustrated in the formation of the Community Health Foundation of Cleveland (CHF) in the mid-1960s. Here, a physician with prepaid group practice experience formed a new medical corporation before the plan became operational. New physicians were recruited to an organization owned by a sole proprietor. It was understood that the proprietor would establish for the group working procedures based on prepaid group practice principles. When the group became familiar with the new format, the organization would be coverted from sole proprietorship to a partnership or some comparable format. Here, then, strong physician leadership solves the medical group organizing paradox.[91]

Consultants working with the Cleveland Community Health Foundation founders called attention to this leadership element:

> In this (matter of physician working hours), as in all other aspects relating to patient care, the fact that the physicians knew that their appointment to

the group was predicated on their initial acceptance of the work rules presented to them by the medical director and his associate, made consolidation of the effort possible. Many problems which in other groups have invited debate into the early hours of the morning were never on the agenda of this group. As they developed their own experience, they questioned some of the rules, modified some, and abandoned some that appeared to be inapplicable to the CHF situation.

The essential contribution of firm leadership at the outset was to establish a way of life geared to good patient care.[92]

Leadership, then, creates a viable organizational culture—a way of life.

THE HEALTH MAINTENANCE ISSUE

Finally, the physician leader not only helps to resolve the operational problems of group recruitment and practice, but he also addresses the basic policy issues that his group and prepaid group practice face in today's turbulent environment. One such issue is embedded in the *HMO* term which carries a promise: People will be kept healthy. Yet many health problems that befall us are not "fixable" by traditional, curative medical practices. So the term names an issue, not a solution. This health maintenance issue is part of the traditional physician perspective:

Many patients come to doctors with problems for which the doctor has no solution. Unhappiness, inability to love with one's mate, alcoholism, juvenile delinquency, sexual deviations, poverty, illiteracy, and drug dependency are not usually helped by the doctor. These are problems which relate to the entire society and they do not have medical solutions . . . Most of the time, no treatable disease is discovered and the patient or third party pays a high bill for what might be called negative medicine.[93]

Dr. Cutting of the Kaiser-Permanente program suggests that the prepaid group practice format has an intrinsic incentive to address this issue:

If indeed everyone is better off if our members remain well, we must continually strive for more substantive measures with which to accomplish prevention and early recognition of disease. This is closely related to experimentation in new delivery systems, uses of paramedical personnel for health screening, and evaluation in health education. It is becoming even more related to habits and lifestyles of the public than to expertness in the science of medicine.[94]

Prepaid group practice, then, accepts responsibility for "negative medicine"—more constructively called illness prevention and/or health promotion—and, unlike traditional medical practice, the group is in a position to negotiate with the consumers how their economic investment in health care is to be divided between curative and promotive benefits. HMO involvement by physicians and hospitals immediately raises two other basic issues: If physicians in the HMO format are encouraged to be cost conscious—think like managers—whose agents are they—the company's or the patient's? If hospital managers are to be entrepreneurs, they must face up to the fundamental things being risked—their organization's credibility as community service institutions and their organization's very existence if they guess wrong about emerging market realities.

NOTES

Chapter 4

1. Peter F. Drucker, *Managing In Turbulent Times* (London: Pan Books, 1981), pp. 9–10.

2. "Will Hospitals Close?", *AMA News*, June 24, 1983, p. 3.

3. Jeff C. Goldsmith, *Can Hospitals Survive?* (Homewood, Ill: Dow Jones-Irwin, 1981), p. xv.

4. Ibid., pp. 97–98.

5. Ibid., pp. 101–102.

6. Ibid., p. 104.

7. Ibid., p. 105.

8. Ibid., p. 107. (Italics added)

9. Ibid., p. 154. (Italics added)

10. Ibid., pp. 180–81. (Italics added)

11. Ibid., p. 105.

12. Ibid., pp. 148 and 152–54.

13. "Hospital Administrators Seek Medical Staff Cooperation," *AMA News*, March 18, 1983, p. 1.

14. Ibid.

15. Ibid. p. 6.

16. "Physicians' Roles in Corporations Debated," *AMA News*, March 18, 1983, p. 6.

17. Ibid., p. 7.

18. Michael E. Porter, "How Competitive Forces Shape Strategy," *Harvard Business Review*, March–April 1979, p. 145.

19. Ibid.

20. Ibid., p. 143.

21. Faith B. Rafkind, *Hospital Competitive Adaptation Strategy*, Masters' Thesis, Sloan School of Management, Massachusetts Institute of Technology, 1982, p. 76.

22. Porter, "Competitive Forces," p. 142.

23. "Lines Getting Blurred Between M.D.s, Hospitals," *AMA News,* June 24, 1983, p. 14.

24. Goldsmith, *Can Hospitals Survive?* pp. 16–17.

25. Gail Warden and Edward Tuller, "HMOs and Hospitals: What Are the Options," *Hospitals,* August 16, 1979, p. 64.

26. Linda Burns, "Lessons Learned through Hospital Involvement in HMOs," *Hospitals,* August 16, 1979, p. 77.

27. Jan Malcolm and Paul M. Ellwood, Jr., M.D., "Competitive Approach May Ease Problems in Delivery System," *Hospitals,* August 16, 1979, pp. 67–68.

28. "Private Sector Investment in Health Maintenance Organizations: A Case Study of Hospital Sponsorship" (Rockville, Md.: Department of Health and Human Services, Publication no. PHS 82-50183, June 1982), p. 1.

29. Goldsmith, *Can Hospitals Survive?* p. xv.

30. "Private Sector," p. 11.

31. James D. Campbell, M.D., "Hospitals and Physicians," in *Proceedings of the Twenty-Third Annual George Bugbee Symposium* (Chicago: Center for Health Administration Studies, June 1981), p. 84.

32. Ibid., p. 82.

33. "Private Sector," p. 2.

34. "Are There a New Set of HMO Sponsors in the Wings?" *Group Health News,* March 1983, p. 2.

35. Marvin R. Weisbord, "Why Organization Development Hasn't Worked (so far) in Medical Centers," *Health Care Management Review,* Spring 1976, p. 17.

36. Ibid., p. 20.

37. George Maddox and Eugene Stead, M.D.s, "The Professional and Citizen Participation," in *Proceedings of the 1973 Duke University Hospital Forum* (Durham: Duke University, 1973), p. 74.

38. J. A. Morton, *Organizing for Innovation* (New York: McGraw-Hill, 1971), pp. 34–36.

39. Weisbord, "Organizational Development," p. 20.

40. Drucker, *Managing,* p. 189.

41. Cecil Cutting, M.D., "Historical Development and Operating Concept" in *The Kaiser-Permanente Medical Care Program,* ed. Anne Sommers (New York: Commonwealth Fund, 1971), p. 21.

42. Morton, *Organizing,* p. 35.

43. Ibid.

44. Ibid., p. 36.

45. Gene Bylinsky, "Can Bell Labs Keep It Up?" *Fortune,* June 27, 1983, p. 90.

46. Phillip Chu, M.D., "Remarks on Alternative Delivery Systems," delivered at Blue Cross Association meeting on Alternative Forms of Health Care Finance and Delivery," Kansas City, 1970, p. 1.

47. Ibid., p. 2.

48. Ernest S. Saward, M.D., "The Role of the Medical Director in the Group Practice HMO," presented at a conference on The Medical Director in Prepaid Group Practice Health Maintenance Organizations, Denver, 1973.

49. Greer Williams, "Kaiser," *Modern Hospital,* February 1971, p. 77.

50. Weisbord, "Organization Development," p. 20.

51. H. L. Light and R. K. Match, "The Potential of the Teaching Hospital for the Development of Prepaid Group Practices," *Medical Care* 14 no. 8 (August 1976), pp. 643–53. This section puts this excellent case study into the role-innovator framework.

52. Maddox, "The Professional," pp. 71–72.

53. Quoted in Thomas R. O'Donovan, "The Primary Care Initiative," *The Journal of Ambulatory Care Management,* February 1981, pp. 34–35.

54. Burns, "Lessons," p. 74.

55. Ibid., p. 75.

56. Bruce Steinhauer, M.D., "HMO Impact on Hospitals: The Possibilities and Realities," in *Prepaid Health Plans* (Chicago: Chicago Hospital Council, 1983), p. 26.

57. Ibid., p. 26.

58. Ibid., p. 25.

59. Ibid., pp. 27–28.

60. This section puts Rafkind's brilliant case study into a role innovation framework. Rafkind's study is easily the best one on the organizational process by which a hospital pursues HMO involvement in today's competitive environment.

61. Rafkind, *Hospital,* p. 225.

62. Ibid., p. 236.

63. Ibid., p. 252.

64. Ibid., p. 227.

65. Ibid., p. 242.

66. Ibid., p. 215.

67. Ibid., pp. 214–15.

68. Ibid., p. 228.

69. Ibid., p. 230.

70. Ibid., p. 231.

71. Ibid.

72. Ibid., p. 240.

73. Ibid., p. 263.

74. Ibid., pp. 238–39.

75. Ibid., p. 241.

76. Ibid., p. 233.

77. Ibid., p. 253.

78. Ibid., p. 255.

79. Ibid.

80. Avram Yedidia, *Planning and Implementation of the Community Health Foundation* (Washington, D.C.: PHS–HEW, 1969), p. 2.

81. Chu, "Remarks," p. 3.

82. Ibid.

83. Conrad Rosenberg, M.D., "Physician Responsibility and Cooperative Planning," delivered at Blue Cross Association Conference on HMO Planning, New Orleans, 1975, pp. 1–2.

84. Robert Match, M.D., "The Keystone of the HMO: Its Medical Director," presented at a Conference on the Medical Director in Prepaid Group Practice HMOs, Denver, 1973, p. 2.

85. Rosenberg, "Physician Responsibility," p. 1.

86. Saward, "The Role of the Medical Director." p. 2.

87. Ibid., p. 5.

88. Quoted in Betsy Weal, "Northcare: HMO with Promise," *Modern Health Care,* June, 1975, p. 65.

89. Quoted in W. P. Deering and I. Miller, *The Role of Physician Leadership* (Chicago: Blue Cross Association, 1975), p. 4.

90. David O. Ottensmeyer, M.D., "Lessons from an HMO Launching," *Group Practice,* October 1973, p. 30.

91. See "Recruitment of Physicians and Organization of the Medical Group" in Yedidia, *Planning and Implementation,* Chapter X.

92. Ibid., p. 69.

93. Maddox, p. 76.

94. Cecil Cutting, M.D., "Reflections of a Medical Director" (Oakland, Calif.: Kaiser-Permanente Advisory Service, October 1976, p. 12.

∎5

Citizen health care activism
in turbulent times

ENTREPRENEURSHIP AND ACTIVISM: SIX POINTS

∎ Citizen activism, like its payer and provider counterparts, grows in turbulent times. The emerging health care mentality, therefore, must include an understanding of consumer activism. Odin Anderson puts the challenge this way: "The awareness and influence of consumers is sure to increase. Can management tap their influence constructively?"[1] This challenge is the fourth managerial mandate in turbulent times—working with the rising consumer. Like the three mandates listed by Goldsmith, this one points toward cooperation. Again, the survival curve point is that while necessity is the mother of innovation, cooperation acts as the midwife. As Walter J. McNerney has noted, groups are building local coalitions around all sorts of issues as people cease looking to Washington for answers to social problems.[2] Moreover, this surge of activism is marked by an overall strategy of negotiation and compromise.

This citizen movement can be seen in the example of a Boston neighborhood's relationship with a Harvard Medical School hospital construction project. The example shows that hospitals and citizen coalitions can work together toward a more diverse, accountable, and affordable health care system—a "health care system on a hill." In 1970, Harvard wanted to build a tertiary hospital in Boston's Mission Hill neighborhood. Residents found this disruptive and unresponsive to their community's health care needs. They blocked construction for a decade. Finally, Harvard accepted a negotiated solution and conceded to three consumer demands—the new hospital would have a substantial primary care operation, its board would include community residents, and demolished housing at the new hospital site would be replaced. Two further consumer demands were met in the Mission Hill area: First, the Harvard Community Health Plan, an HMO originally sponsored by the university and designed for a middle-class, professional clientele, established an outpost in the working-class and poor Mission Hill area. So now, Mission Hill residents have a health coverage alternative. Second, the community recruited a young general practitioner (GP) to practice humanistic, relatively low-technology medicine.[3]

The first lesson to be learned from this example is pointed out by Peter Drucker—the hospital, like all institutions in a turbulent, pluralistic society, has become a political institution. It is defined by its constituencies. According to Drucker, "A 'constituency' is a group that can impede an institution and can veto its decisions . . . [Its] opposition is a genuine threat to the institution's capacity to perform and to its very survival."[4] The second lesson—one that goes beyond Drucker's negative view of constituencies—is that local citizen coalitions can get institutions to act (have an HMO establish a satellite) and can initiate programs themselves (recruit a humanistic GP).

A third lesson is that citizen groups show an increasingly sophisticated understanding of economic development and negotiation. As reported recently, neighborhood groups and economic developers around the country are increasingly finding cooperation to be mutually advantageous. Echoing many of Iaccoca's survival curve themes, local coalitions are talking about pursuing neighborhood survival by means of public-private partnership deals negotiated into place. Marshall Ingwerson has identified a national shift in climate from confrontational to more cooperative relationships among business people, neighborhoods, and city government officials as communities strive to compete for industrial development ventures which create jobs and increase local tax bases. The key to this shift to conciliation is that these partnerships are understood as calculated business deals concerning common interests. These deals are constructed by hard-headed negotiations with the best deals often being negotiated by the toughest citizen coalitions whose leaders are realistic and understand the other side's perspective.[5] Ingwerson provides an illustration of the changing situation:

> "When I first got into politics about 20 years ago," says William S. Taupier,
> . . . "you almost had to be antibusiness."
> Mr. Taupier, a former mayor of Holyoke, Massachusetts, recalls a typical complaint at a city council meeting that a builder wanted a zoning change "just so he can make money."
> "Excuse me," Taupier said, "but why else should he want a zoning change?"
> In other words, negotiators on both sides of the table need to think like businessmen; businessmen need to think like politicians.[6]

A fourth lesson is that as Washington withdraws funding and leadership, local groups will expect local payers and hospitals to be cooperative partners in solving local health care problems. Failure to respond to this expectation of catalytic leadership from its community constituencies will deny the hospital the loyalty of these groups. This can hurt marketing severely. It can, as Harvard learned, lead to these groups trying to block hospital efforts to pursue paths to expansion and corporatization. Perhaps more important, as they begin to look like businesses, hospitals will face the crisis in legitimacy that has confronted the American corporation in recent years. Politically this could be ruinous, for as an American Hospital Association official once suggested, we have not seen National Health Insurance here because the American hospital is the beneficiary of an enormous pool of community loyalty. People do not want to see "their hospital" run by Washington. As hospitals become part of large corporations, this protection will be eroded unless hospitals work to maintain local loyalty. In short, loyal constituencies can protect institutions in turbulent times. Thus, if hospitals want consumers to believe that they are getting their money's worth, and if medical societies want consumers to think that medical practices and technologies yield better health, then both hospitals and organized medicine will need more than effective public relations campaigns. The new entrepreneurs will have to be coalition builders.

Edward J. Connors, president of Sisters of Mercy Health Corporation, adds a fifth point. Active citizen participation in multihospital systems "is a strength to be maintained." Moreover, he contends that multihospital systems actually have some advantages in terms of making hospital governance work.[7] A sixth point is that deregulation of an industry invites increased consumer activism. Ralph Nader recently proposed a set of reforms for the now deregulated airline industry. Modeled after reforms in the utility field, these ideas could easily be applied in a procompetition-structured health care field. His ideas include:

Each ticket, policy, or bill would have information on how to join an airline passenger association.

This association would largely deal with complaints.

Each member would vote for a governing council.

The association would hire experts.

It would, in general, guard the interests of policy holders/users.

It would be not-for-profit.

It would follow successful precedents, such as the Wisconsin Citizen's Utility Board.[8]

The task, then, of hospitals in a competitive world is not only to win customers, but also to enlist constituencies.

THE CHALLENGE OF POLITICAL INTEGRATION

Community action and participation, from the consumer activist point of view, is simply an expression of the Jeffersonian belief in democracy, which implies that people should be able to knowledgeably participate in basic decisions that shape their lives. According to G. M. Hochbaum, an advocate of consumer participation:

> Segments of our population, which until recently have played a passive role, are demanding full and equal access to all resources and services that our society is capable of providing. For a person it is not enough to be given what he wants. He feels an urge to have something to say about *what* is given, *where*, and in *what ways* it is given. He wants to know that he has at least some control over such things which, after all, affect his health and welfare and his very life.[9]

Moreover, activists do not want to feel that their participation is simply something that they are merely entitled to, but something that can help make their health care system better and more responsive to their informed expectations about cost and quality. Faced by activated community groups that want to negotiate coalitions for constructive action, the hospital manager as social entrepreneur must see himself as a leader who is a *political integrator* in Mary Parker Follett's sense of the term. This is part of the new entrepreneurial mentality.

Peter Drucker summarizes this view of the hospital manager as political conciliator, activist, and integrator:

> The new manager . . . will be effective only if he ceases to see himself—and to be seen—as representing a "special interest" role . . . He can no longer depend on the political process to be the integrating force, he himself has to become the integrator . . . And this means that the manager has to think through what the policy should be in the general interest and to provide social cohesion.[10]

Morris Janowitz carries this logic a step further. He suggests that if we are to get our economy moving again, we must involve citizens in the governance and management of local service institutions.[11]

DEBATING CONSUMER PARTICIPATION

Although some health care leaders may see the need for building a consumer constituency, they may still resist. Here are three objections which may be raised in the activism debate. Each is discussed.

Consumerism is a hassle

Our appreciation of innovations like consumer participation is often shaped by historic dramatic announcements of legislative initiatives which promise massive social change. Snags befall these projects which are aimed at implementing the grandiose legislative goals. The pattern of first reporting bold legislative promises and then bemoaning faltering local performance is occasionally broken by exceptions to the rules which are covered in the magazine section of the Sunday newspaper. There we find "rare" stories of programs that have met adversity but made real headway. While these stories may preserve hope, they do not erase the main message—expect failure. Still, rarely do we hear about why innovations fail. People find it easier to blame the innovation for failure rather than to learn how to implement new concepts effectively.

In the volatile 1960s, a push for mandatory citizen participation came from the federal government. Public policy was to encourage "maximum feasible participation" for poor people in social and health care programs. Michael Lipsky and Morris Lounds, in an excellent review of this power-over approach to citizen action, identify a basic contradiction in programs that emerged in the 1960s.[12] Citizen participation was not allowed to evolve naturally in response to local cultures, circumstances, problems, and strengths. Rather, it had to respond first and foremost to changing pressures from federal grantors and local sponsors. The demand on local projects, according to Lipsky's and Lounds's analysis, was for the quick and visible display of "citizen-participants." Typically, a project director met this demand by initially overselling to the community the program's potential benefits and the extent of community control over the program. At the same time, the director would underemphasize the difficulty of achieving long-term financial viability. These tactics proved effective in recruiting "instant" community councils, but were ruinous in terms of true institution building. Instead of one objective—accountable, effective programs—this test of citizen participation separated symbolic participation from actual program performance. This eroded both participation and performance. It led to rancorous conflicts. Building a real consumer constituency and agreement building calls for more than salesmanship and symbolic gestures. Symbolic participation as a mandatory, rancorous hassle is an unneeded myth.

We cannot find real consumers

Once the negative stereotypes and contradictions of mandatory participation are overcome, we need to identify the consumer. Some health care leaders argue that once a person is a board member, he is no longer a real consumer. But as we have shown in the case of manager and provider role innovators, what is required to make an innovation work and voluntary action succeed is not a pristine person, but rather a boundary rider who is able to represent one cultural viewpoint to people with other cultural viewpoints. Though it is hard to keep constituency foremost in the mind, the problem is no greater for the consumer representative than it is for the role innovative manager or provider who must also bridge cultures. The "real consumer" is an unneeded myth.

It gets bogged down

Another debate point against consumer participation is how to keep the democratic process from getting bogged down in difficult logistical problems. Organizations often give this logistical task low priority and inadequate resources. The manager who is assigned this responsibility is in a position of inviting people to a party and then not having any time, money, and so on to prepare for the party and entertain the people. His only hope is that democracy will spontaneously arise. This is unfortunate because in order to become a better informed and responsible citizen with regard to health care delivery and financing, the citizen/consumer needs the encouragement and expertise of the manager. The knowledge and skills of the manager are primary resources for the citizen/consumer in his efforts to become effective.

Moreover, an invitation to cooperative voluntary action must have a sound and hospitable follow through. After reviewing many HEW studies on citizen participation and reflecting on his own direct experiences, Elliot Richardson made the following points about participatory hospitality:

> Much depends on the form and availability of the participation as well as on the citizens' perception of its impact. If participation involves going to meetings, the convenience of their times and places will make a difference. . . . The opportunity to be heard may be adequate, but that isn't worth much if nobody listens. The authorities may listen, promise to do something, but consistently fail to follow through. They may listen but decline—for good reasons or bad— to accept the citizens' views.[13]

Thus, participation can be effectively handled if adequate thought, knowledge, skills, time, resources, and so on are committed to get the job done, and if the consumer's contribution and stake are respected and honestly accepted. The myth of democracy being either too cumbersome or too easy is an unneeded myth.

PREPAID GROUP PRACTICE: CONSUMER PARTICIPATION AND VOLUNTARY ACTION

Prepaid group practices, by definition, rely on consumers; that is, prepaid group practices are organizations serving, and responsible to, known populations of consumers by means of a defined set of providers within fixed budgets. Members have a yearly choice between staying with the program and leaving it. This definition calls attention to the heart of excellent health care delivery— the cooperative interrelationship of subscriber, provider, and manager constituencies.

The program's purpose and budget gathers these constituencies together. These groups cannot, however, work together effectively as allies unless they also include in their cultural framework an active awareness of operating in a world of scarce resources. Though each group is influenced by its own needs and imperatives, the budget holds them together. Hence, whenever members involved in governance have participated in deliberations, it always had to be in the acknowledged context of a defined budget. Consumers in the prepaid group practice movement have quickly learned that there are no "free lunches" in health care services—the budget constrains provider, manager, and consumer constituencies alike.

The consumer, then, is a member of a defined population for which the organization and its management have assumed some responsibilities. This means that the PGP is less like an insurance company which merely reacts to customer economic needs on an individual after-the-fact basis (pays a bill), and more like a public school district that makes prearrangements for services to enhance its "public" (builds and maintains schools). In other words, the prepaid group practice consumer public is more than an abstract group of individuals holding separate insurance policies—they rub shoulders in an actual institution. As members, they share a concrete life situation at the health center. Moreover, by being members, subscribers are legally assured and expect service. These two qualities—a public that is aware and a responsible organization—are ideal cultural structural conditions for consumer voluntary action and program accountability.

Finally, the existence of the health insurance option—dual choice—can lead to consumer participation. *Dual choice* means the consumer has an annual opportunity to choose between types of health coverage. If he selects the prepaid group practice program, many decisions, which under traditional health insurance arrangements would be made by him in the marketplace, are "predecided" by the three constituencies through their negotiation of the fixed budget. In turn, if these "predecisions" are unsatisfactory, the consumer can "vote with his feet" during the dual-choice period by leaving the program. Or, if satisfied, the "entitled" member can participate in the predecisions.

Paul Starr has compared the advantages that prepaid group practice has over health system agencies (HSAs) when it comes to making citizen participation work.[14] He compares these two systems in terms of three political variables: accountability, participation, and representation. *Accountability* means X is answerable to Y who controls some resource (money, votes, and so on) vital to X. *Participation* refers to the levels of activities that Elliot Richardson listed. *Representation* carries with it the rejection of direct democracy in favor of some mediating group. In HSAs, Starr argues, consumers have no resources with which to control their representatives. As for participation, it is the providers who have the most at stake in HSAs. They are the most aroused participants and have the most resources. Representation under the HSA scheme is an abstract anticonsumer-constituency approach where people are selected because they represent a community's demographic profile. In a consumer-owned prepaid group practice, such as Seattle's Group Health Cooperative, Starr notes that consumer representatives are elected to the governing board by the membership and can be voted out of office. Participation is possible through an intricate system of committees and task forces as well as board positions. Representatives to the board, Starr argues, are atypical in commitment and skills, and elected on their merit. Finally, at least some members are aroused since they have to pay for board decisions.

LEADERSHIP AS FACILITATING PRAGMATIC PROBLEM SOLVING

There is a 20th century tradition of neighborhood health and community centers which emphasize citizen participation. Some of these early neighborhood centers were innovative in a fashion startlingly similar to today's initiatives. Wilbur Phillips, in 1916, pioneered a community-based, prevention-oriented health center in Cincinnati where residents were used as outreach workers. Moreover, the center's board was made up of representatives elected by each block in the community as well as an equal number of experts and professionals drawn from the district as a whole. This board defined the project's focus on preventive health care services.[15] Phillips viewed the project as an experiment in democracy. Its purpose was "to promote a type of democratic community organization through which the citizenship as a whole can participate directly in the control of community affairs while at the same time making constant use of the highest skill available."[16] He believed that citizen participation was not counter to effectiveness, but rather was a principal contributor to program viability that helped to assure responsiveness to need and usage of service. As opposed to the confrontation tactics of the 1960s, this early neighborhood health center focused on a pragmatic power-with problem-solving approach.

The program achieved widespread community participation both in program governance and in utilization. It faltered after three years, however, when the city's mayor attacked it on ideological grounds as being "a step from bolshevism." This reflected the program's autonomy from traditional city machine politics and organized medicine. Overall, the program was judged by observers of the day as promising in its performance. Of course, citizen-governed health centers did not take over medical care in America. Neighborhood health centers, where they existed, were more often "bureaucratically run by municipal health departments and voluntary agencies."[17] Nonetheless, efforts like the Cincinnati experiment sustained the citizen-governed neighborhood center movement as a workable alternative institution.

Mary Parker Follet's basic ground rules for negotiated cooperation were derived in part from her study of citizen participation in the Cincinnati health center. These rules have been obeyed in the governance of the nation's largest consumer-sponsored prepaid group practice programs as is characterized by some statements by its leaders:

Perhaps the outstanding attribute of the co-op has been the development of a close working relationship between the members of the consumer-staff-management team. Disagreements are commonplace and openly expressed . . . but we are accustomed to working long and hard for rational and harmonious solutions.[18]

We really negotiate as equals, each with responsibilities and priorities in his own area and each has to ultimately accommodate itself to the other's priorities. We haven't found it profitable or reasonable to try to resolve professional-lay decisions by anyone having the final word and saying, "this, or else."[19] Visitors often comment on the esprit de corps which permeates the organization.[20]

Many of us have worked in volunteer capacities in various activities and usually one comes and goes. . . . Most volunteers are not really fully involved in the organizations they are working for. . . . That has not been true at group health. The board and its various committees and other persons, some 200 in the total leadership corps, stay involved not only because it matters to us, but because we have an effect—what we decide, what we think, matters.[21]

These collaborative points are strikingly similar to the lessons learned in the Boston-area, hospital-based individual practice association (IPA) venture.

MAXIMUM FEASIBLE PARTICIPATION: PROBLEMS OF A POWER-OVER PROCESS

A Power-over model

Federally funded community health centers of the 1960s had participation problems partly because of a power-over approach. It can benefit the consumer leader to learn from the lessons of these federally funded health programs. The planning process at these centers was conflict laden. It typically had four phases:[22]

1. *Cosmetic community.* The sponsoring organization enlisted "community" leaders to meet federal regulations. Potential conflicts in values and interests between the sponsor (research) and the community (better access) were deemphasized.[23] Since participation was mandated, little care was directed to consider substantive reasons for sponsor-community collaboration.

2. *Disappointment.* The community "leaders" learned that the sponsor would not support their ideas. They discovered that their leadership was merely cosmetic, not substantive. Consumer roles, resources, and responsibili-

ties were poorly defined. Consumer-professional communications broke down with each party having little understanding of the other's culture.[24]

3. *Things fall apart.* Contradictions suppressed in Step 1 and clarified in Step 2 now rose to the surface as overt conflict over some issue. A power-over struggle for control of the venture broke out.[25] These disputes went in two directions—management pushed for consumer involvement as an administrative top-down tool—a consumer marketing/complaint system, and grass roots activists pushed for converting the project into a political tool for changing the community.[26] The goal of an effective consumer-based health care program was lost in both cases. They were compromises in Follett's sense that the problem was not solved.

4. *Institution building.* An effective organization backed by an active, loyal constituency is achieved.

A prepaid group practice power-over example

Many prepaid group practice efforts in the last 15 years have attempted consumer participation. Sometimes, however, past lessons learned have been ignored in building consumer participation much as they have been in manager and provider development. Implementation mistakes have been repeated, and the concept of participation has undeservedly been tarnished.

In the 1970s, the development of the Columbia Medical Plan prepaid group practice sponsored by the Johns Hopkins Medical Institution demonstrated key ingredients of the "cosmetic community" concept. The sponsoring institution's purpose for prepaid group practice development was to provide training and research opportunities to its students. The plan's administrator, concerned with funding and community acceptance, instigated a consumer advisory council. He reports: "During the early feasibility planning period . . . we had a concept of involving the consumer in some way."[27] This way was not, however, spelled out.

Since this middle-class consumer council lacked a defined role, it spent its first year educating itself about prepaid group practice in general and the Columbia Plan specifically, defining its role, and organizing itself to represent plan enrollees. This "cosmetic community" presented to funding sources was actually conflict laden, having a sponsor with its own agenda and citizen participants without clear objectives or purpose.

Columbia moved to the second phase—"disappointment."

> The consumer council became increasingly aware of the insensitivity of the board of trustees to the attitudes and concerns of consumers of the Columbia Medical Plan; and the council became increasingly aware that management was not soliciting its advice and counsel on *significant* policy matters.[28]

In short, the council found the board unresponsive to its efforts to play a substantive policy role. Sponsor priorities dominated the program and left little role and/or decision making to consumers.

In Columbia, the "things fall apart" stage represented a turn to "administrative participation." A crisis happened in the council's second year. Its efforts to have a knowledgeable say in the control of the plan were discouraged and ignored. When council's sole representative on the plan's board resigned in protest, the council began to question the reason for its very existence. Afterward, the council worked to define a role for itself acceptable to the board. "It appears to have been more active, but in less significant matters." With no real responsibility or resources, the council accepted an administrative participation role for the time being, helping the plan sell itself to the community.[29]

From this experience, we see that there are at least four things that must be built into any effort to create substantive consumer participation: clearly defined *roles,* adequate *resources* to prepare the participants for these roles, *responsiveness* from the sponsoring institution so that it is clear that everyone believes in the value of participation; and negotiating *rules* when roles clash and conflict has to be resolved. These doings, havings, and thinkings constitute an organizational culture conducive to effective consumer participation.

STEPS AND ROLES OF A POWER-WITH PROCESS

Here I will discuss a 10-step power-with approach to consumer-sponsored HMO formation. For this community network process to be successful, it is necessary that consumer leaders effectively play a set of team roles. The steps and roles were used in the Hyde Park–Kenwood Health Task Force's HMO enterprise in Chicago.

Process

1. *Impetus: Kindle discontent.*
The process began with a housewife who was discontent with the current local health care situation. She and a few others felt that health care in Hyde Park had grown too complex, fragmented, and problematic. They believed that the values of scientific medicine and bureaucratic organization needed to be balanced by increased attention to the value of personalism— treating the whole person and not merely one or more diseased organs.

2. *Seek an actionable answer.*
Quickly a small group of like-minded people—the founders—gathered to educate themselves about health care, its problems, and its solutions. Though inexperienced in the health care field, the founders were experienced in citizen action. Articles from respected publications, such as *Fortune* and *Scientific American,* offered the beginnings of a common library on the topic. Administrators of innovative health care programs were contacted and visited. The founders talked with friends and neighbors, and from the beginning sought

advice from concerned local physicians and hospital personnel at the University of Chicago.

The process was open and involving. It was viewed as a pragmatic venture in problem solving and institution building. The key criterion was pragmatic idealism. The Hyde Parkers eschewed confrontation with established institutions—they sought cooperation. As was the case in Rochester, a concrete, actionable health care delivery alternative—prepaid group practice—was chosen.

3. *Get a strategically-located patron.*

After the founders decided on a specific alternative, they needed a strategically placed organizational beachhead or enclave and a modest number of resources. The Hyde Park–Kenwood Community Conference, a 20-year-old community organization, responded favorably to the founders' action proposal and offered help by way of office space, support, contacts with key organizations and people, and a simple endorsement of the founders' proposal. This beachhead enabled the venture to mature. The founders refined their ideas for action through the development of foundation and federal grant proposals. The community organization's director became the HMO's innovation patron.

4. *Establish a decision-making structure.*

The Hyde Parkers had a shared sense of founding something new—of constitution making. The development of an innovative health care institution provided a common purpose which in turn provided the source of authority—not tradition (physician authority), not rationality (bureaucratic rules), and not charisma (some visionary leader). The unfolding venture itself was authoritative. In this step, the *basic values* (for example, citizen governance, personalism) of the founders were reaffirmed in stated operating principles. A new organizational culture began to emerge. The group adopted some formal organizational shape and membership as it became a task force of the community organization. This task force gained a measure of visibility and legitimacy in the community by adding strategic people to its membership. They came, in part, through the sponsor's interorganizational network. Most of these members were *not* community power brokers. Some, however, were well known and respected by such brokers. Some were health care experts, including physicians; others were interested citizens. The venture thereby gained precious skills, perceptions, and access to resources. A grant to hire a planner was obtained from the Illinois Regional Medical Program.

5. *Make decisions and resolve conflict.*

The absence of power brokers reflected the group's dedication to pragmatic problem solving instead of a confrontational approach to convert their beliefs into a concrete program. Also, the roles of the founders and the strategic people were clarified by formal documents, such as the operating principles, as well as bylaws, structure, and operations. For example, the founders became the task force's steering committee. This step was very stressful as ideals became defined operationally, and conflict broke out at this point in the process. The task force's one charismatic leader and the community organization's president had a power struggle for control of the project. The original planner took sides and was fired. A replacement (the author) was hired. Cooperative resolution depended on the common purpose—the *law of the situation*—being given renewed priority over ideological differences. The charismatic leader resigned, and a new power-with leader emerged.

6. *Organize for work.*

The task force was a working one. It formed committees to address functional areas, such as financial planning, marketing, and the medical system. This work further educated the members, and demonstrated dedication and ability to potential medical staff members as well as to potential funding sources. Team leadership and specific roles necessary for effective work and decision making emerged. Moreover, because Hyde Park is a university town, the planner was able to tap an extended information network including the Blue Cross Association, Group Health Association of America (GHAA), and the University of Chicago.

7. *Reinvent the solution and choose an ally.*

A consumer-governed prepaid group practice plan consists of three parts: a medical group practice, a plan administration, and a consumer governing body. Development of any of these components is a major undertaking. The Hyde Park group faced a key decision concerning whether or not to revise their strategic decisions by developing an alliance with an existing organization which had the capacity to develop one or two of these components. To decide this issue, they made a realistic appraisal of the feasibility of their proposed program, their own capability, and the responsiveness of any potential ally. The task force elected to focus on developing a quality, community-owned health center that would negotiate with network model HMOs in order to deliver care to their prepaid subscribers. Once it persuaded the local Blue Cross Plan of its commitment to be an HMO delivery outlet, Blue Cross gave the venture a very timely $10,000 grant. The Hyde Parkers and the Blue Cross Plan had successfully negotiated entrepreneurial roles.

8. *Community enterprise.*

As development of the group program proceeded, it grew increasingly technical. Experts were needed to assist the project. Gradually, the administrative and medical-nursing staffs took over much of the burden of technical work, with the task force shaping policy and assessing technical systems proposed by the professionals. Board skills and outside technical assistance were used to fill gaps. Considerable money was needed to house and launch an ambulatory care center. Funds were raised from the Robert Wood Johnson Foundation, a local bond drive, a local bank loan, and a line of credit. The bonds paid the same 5 percent interest rate as did local banks' savings accounts. The idea was to be entrepreneurial but not too entrepreneurial. Hence citizens were encouraged to invest—to risk their money—but not to expect to profit greatly.

9. *Startup.*

The first years of the program's operation were difficult as it strove to reach the financial break-even point while staying loyal to the original goals. Slowly, the original founders stepped aside allowing new leaders to emerge. The program stabilized and assumed its place among the community's established institutions. Tension, however, mounted over whether the new institution was just another bureaucracy.

10. *Add value: Changing the community's health care culture*

The task force (now the center's board) reaffirmed its dedication to a basic value—concern for the whole person—and devoted resources to shaping its program in response to this value. Further, it moved outward into the community and strove to influence the community's culture to emphasize this value. Several of the original founders played a key role in this renewal of purpose. It is this sense of founding something new, of framing a new constitution of things, and a consensus of values that is perhaps the citizens' greatest potential contribution to the voluntary health care field. Citizens can insist that certain self-evident truths be constructively held; that is, put into action. This reassertion of first principles is a revolutionary act in the American sense—a revolving back to basic ideals.

Roles

Citizen action is group action. Effective citizen voluntarism in health care depends, then, on making groups work well. In Hyde Park, we stressed building effective group dynamics. A model perfected by T. T. Patterson, one of England's foremost management experts, identifies five basic roles essential for effective group functioning.[30] Applying it to the Hyde Park experience is helpful.

1. *The Excentric role:* For a group to work well it needs input—ideas, data, and so on—from the environment. The one who does this plays the Excentric (away from the center) role. As a recognized role, it allows the group to tolerate new information as well as the person who provides it. The planner was the prime scout for the Hyde Park group, but his message had to be validated and translated to the consumer group by the group's consumer Excentric. This corresponds to the innovation manager or a young Turk.

2. *The Exdominus role:* This role concerns the group's relations with other groups in its environment. As the group's spokesperson, he or she steps forward to implement decisions, often in a bellicose or vociferous fashion. In the Hyde Park situation, the first leader was too charismatic and bellicose— a true "war chief." Since HMO action requires a "peace chief" to conduct

cooperative interorganizational negotiations, he had to be replaced by a person who was less dedicated to fighting ideological enemies and more dedicated to agreement building. This corresponds to the innovation champion.

3. *The Indominus role:* Here the concern is with the group's internal requirements. The Indominus assures parliamentarian-style meetings. He clarifies peoples' roles and makes sure that credit is given for work done. He "knows the ropes" and orients new volunteers. He is in charge of team building. In Hyde Park, the planner's assistant was a local resident who played this role in cooperation with a volunteer Indominus. This volunteer Indominus was dedicated to making her team task- and results-oriented while being very sensitive to peoples' individual feelings and concerns. She would typically say in meetings, "Let's hear him out." Thus, she was the guardian of internal conferring where each issue was fully discussed and everyone listened.

4. *The Exemplar role:* This person crystalizes the group's cultural values by speaking on matters of principle. Seldom bellicose, often quiet and willing to listen, always soaking up the group's moral consensus, he typically says, "I am concerned that if we do this we will be losing sight of why we got into this venture in the first place." More often than not, people around the table agree with his concern. This role in Hyde Park was played by a physicist whose personal, moral response to issues was always remarkably on target. After the first few months of meetings, the group came to recognize his opening words—"I am concerned"—and understood that they had to be very thoughtful about the issue under discussion because valued ideals were at stake.

5. *The Mimetic role:* This role is assumed by group members who follow the other key role players.

Adding to Patterson's list, we had two other roles in the Hyde Park situation.

6. *The Realist role:* We had a 50-year-old business professor who visibly appreciated the group's moral character, but reminded the group that its ideals could only be pursued in the world as it is—one with limited resources, bottom lines, other groups' agendas, and so on.

7. *The Catalyst role:* As planner, I understood my task as striving to assure that all these role players engaged in an effective, value-directed, cooperative process. I championed the process itself. This is what catalytic leadership does.

THE HEALTH MAINTENANCE ISSUE

Prepaid group practices are products of an organizational culture of beliefs and value decisions about what is meant by health care. With the organizational advantages of prepaid group practice come some hazards to what

Elliot Richardson called *personalism*. Nearly 20 years ago, Dr. E. Richard Weinerman asked these questions: Is the conflict between professional and consumer cultures really being addressed? Is the emphasis on high technology and corporate-like organization repulsing the consumer, eroding his loyalty and satisfaction? Is the consumer's demand that he needs care as well as treatment being handled? Do the group's efficiencies impair consumer and physician acceptance? Weinerman believed that consumer acceptance of pre-paid group practice could be improved when patient-physician obstacles are removed, when continuity of care is emphasized, and when attention is given to the whole person. He suggested that service fragmentation could be overcome by a commitment to keeping the whole person in view. After all, it is people and not conditions who seek, accept, and heed medical advice.[31]

In 1981, these issues of the industrialization of health in the HMO field were vividly expressed in Prudential's takeover of the consumer-governed HMO in Evanston, Illinois.[32] The cultural value issues raised by Weinerman, and embedded in the *HMO* term and strategy, emerged with startling clarity. Northcare was a consumer-initiated HMO venture. It was one of the first HMOs to become qualified under the federal HMO Act of 1973. With an excellent medical program, it showed substantial, continuing enrollment growth. Its design, however, suffered from two flaws. Bowing to the founders' ideological commitment to equity of access, the program in its early years had opened enrollment to individuals who were not members of groups. Such people are relatively high users of service. This drove up the expenses of a frail, young company. Also, to get over local physician resistance in the community, the HMO made some costly referral arrangements to outside physician specialists. This concession to provider politics also drove up costs.

The point here is that consumer ideological concerns and professional politics led to a program design that was costly. Unlike Blue Cross in Rochester or Kaiser in Hawaii, the consumers in Evanston simply lacked the capital to pay for design mistakes. Moreover, the physicians in Evanston dealigned from their original coalition with the founding consumers and allied themselves with Prudential and its venture capital. Finally, it must be noted that most Northcare board members approved the buy-out and that a majority of its subscribers voted in favor of the deal.[33] Ironically, the citizen activists had failed over the years to transform the HMO's membership into a loyal constituency. They were risk takers who had not paid enough attention to agreement building.*

---

* As this book goes to press it is interesting to note that Group Health Co-op, a consumer HMO, has just taken over a commercial insurance-owned HMO in Spokane, Washington.

NOTES

Chapter 5

1. Odin W. Anderson, Foreword in Jeff C. Goldsmith, *Can Hospitals Survive?* (Homewood, Ill.: Dow Jones-Irwin, 1981), p. viii.

2. Walter J. McNerney, "Health Care Coalitions," The 1982 Michael M. Davis Lecture delivered at the Center for Health Administration Studies, Chicago, 1982, p. 1.

3. The Malady of Health Care, "NOVA" television series (Boston: WGBN, 1981).

4. Peter F. Drucker, *Managing in Turbulent Times* (London: Pan Books, 1981), p. 203.

5. Marshall Ingwerson, "Cooperation Grows Between Developers, Neighborhood Groups," *Christian Science Monitor,* May 17, 1983, p. 4.

6. Ibid.

7. Edward J. Connors, "Multihospital Systems in the Changing Health Care Landscape," *Trustee,* July 1979, p. 29.

8. Lucian Mouat, "Nader Tries to Get Air Travelers Consumer Group off the Ground," *Christian Science Monitor,* August 6, 1982, p. 6.

9. G. M. Hochbaum, "Consumer Participation in Health Planning: Toward Conceptual Clarification," *American Journal of Public Health* 59, no. 9 (September 1969), p. 1698.

10. Drucker, *Managing,* pp. 212–13.

11. Morris Janowitz, *Social Control of the Welfare State* (New York: Elsevier Scientific Publishing Company, 1976), p. 126.

12. Michael Lipsky and Morris Lounds, "Citizen Participation and Health Care: Problems of Government Induced Participation," *Journal of Health Politics, Policy and Law,* Spring 1976, pp. 85–111.

13. Elliot Richardson, *The Creative Balance* (New York: Holt, Rinehart & Winston, 1976), p. 218.

14. Paul Starr, "Changing the Balance of Power in American Medicine," *Milbank Memorial Fund Quarterly* 58, no. 1 (1980), pp. 167–71.

15. John D. Stoeckle and Lucy M. Candib, "The Neighborhood Health Center—Reform Ideas of Yesterday and Today," *The New England Journal of Medicine* 280, no. 25 (1968), p. 1385.

16. Jesse Frederick Steiner, "The Social Unit Experiment," in *Community Organization in Action,* eds., E. Harper and A. Durham (New York: Association Press, 1959), pp. 121–26.

17. Stoeckle, "Neighborhood Health Center," p. 1387.

18. Lyle Mercer, "The Role of The Member in Group Health Cooperative of Puget Sound," presented at the HMOS Feedback Session, El Paso, Texas, 1972.

19. Aubrey Davis, "Interaction of Board with Medical Staff and Administration," presented at the Prepaid Group Practice School, Seattle, Washington, 1972.

20. Mercer, "The Role of The Member."

21. Davis, "Interaction."

22. Jeoffrey B. Gordon, "The Politics of Community Medicine Projects: A Conflict Analysis," *Medical Care* 7, no. 6 (November–December 1969), p. 422.

23. Jack Elinson and Conrad Herr, "A Sociomedical View of Neighborhood Health Centers," *Medical Care* 8, no. 2 (March–April 1970), p. 98.

24. Milton S. Davis and Robert E. Tranquada, "A Sociological Evaluation of the Watts Neighborhood Health Center," *Medical Care* 7, no. 2 (March–April 1969), p. 106.

25. Ibid.

26. Joseph L. Falkson, *An Evaluation of Alternative Models of Citizen Participation in Urban Bureaucracy* (Ann Arbor: Programs in Health Planning, School of Public Health, University of Michigan, 1971), p. 30.

27. E. Frank Harrelson and Kirk M. Donovan, "Consumer Responsibility in a Prepaid Group Practice Health Plan," *American Journal of Public Health* 65, no. 10 (October 1975), p. 1077.

28. Ibid., p. 1079.

29. Ibid., pp. 1080–83.

30. Humphrey Osmond, M.D., *Understanding Understanding* (New York: Bantam Books, 1974) pp. 173–76. Osmond provides an excellent brief discussion of Patterson's model.

31. E. Richard Weinerman, "Patients' Perceptions of Group Medical Care," *Medical Care,* June 1967, pp. 161–66.

32. Steven Swanson, "Sale of Health Group Poses People versus Profits Issue," *Chicago Tribune,* April 23, 1981.

33. Ibid., p. 1.

∎6
Theory V: The limits of industrialization and the future of voluntarism

MARKETING AND INNOVATION: FROM SURVIVAL TO EXCELLENCE

∎ The hospital world is swiftly becoming consolidated while the variety of health care services increases.[1] Jeff Goldsmith argues that this should happen under the entrepreneurial discipline of the *marketing concept*. He cites Peter Drucker who wrote 30 years ago:

> There is only one valid definition of business purpose: to create a customer.
> Markets are not created by God, nature, or economic forces, but by businessmen. The want they satisfy may have been felt by the customer before he was offered the means of satisfying it. . . But, it was a theoretical want before; only when the action of businessmen makes it effective demand is there a customer, a market.[2]

A marketing orientation is focused, then, on the customer. As Goldsmith puts it, "The marketing concept . . . turns that customer's needs into an organizational mandate."[3] He adds that Theodore Levitt, in his classic *Harvard Business Review* article, "Marketing Myopia," carries the marketing concept one step further. Levitt argues that a business' purpose is not static, but must change with the times. Hence, to be customer oriented becomes, Goldsmith suggests, a mandate for organizational renewal.[4] John Naisbitt points out that Drucker's and Levitt's long-term marketing question—"What business are you in?"—was first raised by Mary Parker Follett with her "Law of Situation." As he recounts: "She had a window shade company as a client and persuaded its owners that they were in the light control business. . . . The Law of Situation asks the question, 'What business are you really in?' "[5]

Levitt, more recently, has carried the marketing concept one step further. He argues that the provision of personal services, such as health care, should

111

be industrialized in the same manner as the production of commodities. His paradigm is McDonald's which he views not as restaurants, but as hamburger factories in the field.[6] Compared to Levitt's radical application of the marketing concept to health care, Goldsmith's thrust is best termed a *semimarketing approach*. On the one hand, Goldsmith sees the health care field as an "industry"[7] with physicians acting as "customer feeders"[8] into health care "corporations."[9] On the other hand, he insists that the hospital's "human values" be preserved,[10] that service is not a "commodity,"[11] and that the hospital is not a "factory."[12]

In his balancing act of traditional and entrepreneurial elements, Goldsmith implicitly recognizes another basic point from Drucker—that marketing is only one of two basic entrepreneurial functions. It is complemented by *innovation*, which Drucker defines as

> the provision of better and more economic goods and services. It is not enough for business to provide any economic goods and services; it must provide better and more economic ones. It is not necessary for a business to grow bigger; but it is necessary that it constantly grow better.[13]

Drucker argues that while only businesses make marketing preeminent, all organizations may innovate; that is, "constantly grow better."[14] In Peters' and Waterman's pursuit of excellence framework, a hospital as an organization may have to market to survive in a competitive environment. But it must innovate in order to excel—to succeed as a value-driven institution.[15] Goldsmith respects this value core of the hospital as a social institution—a community enterprise.

This marketing-innovation distinction is one that reveals an irony in the HMO saga. Dr. Ellwood's institution was in the rehabilitation field. Patients there were sick. He felt a strong professional-moral imperative to help them, and sought an economic-organizational strategy consistent with this imperative. The HMO concept did not, however, focus on aiding the sick, but on keeping people healthy. Given the HMO strategy's marketplace philosophy, it follows that HMOs should merchandise health maintenance. But this runs into a basic professional-moral problem—the medical profession cannot do all that much to keep people healthy. Health is not a commodity produced by providers. People "produce" health. One HMO medical director spoke for many of the field's leaders when he put the issue in innovation versus marketing concept terms:

> I think one of the strongest arguments one can make for an HMO is that it's marketable. But that argument weakens your creditability with the medical staff. We've recruited them to provide effective medical services in an efficient and personal manner. Now are we going to tell them to do what's popular and what will sell? . . . Let's keep the industry taking care of the sick.[16]

From this quotation it is clear that some physicians join HMOs out of its appeal to innovate for excellence. They fear the prospect of being health merchants. Dr. Eric J. Cassell made precisely this point in *The Wall Street Journal*. He argued that our sick care system is the best in the world, but this excellence could be eroded by believing the illusionary claims of those who merchandise health.[17]

Moreover, a vibrant voluntary sector—including the hospital—is an essential dimension of Drucker's voluntary ideal. He cautioned us 30 years ago that the private sector should not take over the functions of the voluntary sector. He wrote: "These are the activities which should be free, that are organized by spontaneous, local, pluralist actions by citizens, not by any one group or governing organ."[18] He warned that if business usurps voluntary sector responsibilities, the response would be "control by the organized government as the representative of the entire people."[19] This is by no means Fourth of July rhetoric. A recent *Business Week* article on the industrialization of the health care field closed with a warning that corporate pursuit of profits and consumer demand for quality may be on a collision course with health care businesses, subject to a massive political backlash.[20] Thus, we have gone full circle. To survive in the marketplace, health care institutions need to become more businesslike; to become too businesslike threatens their success in the political arena.

Drucker's 1954 caveat applies to health care today: "Management is also responsible for making sure that present actions and decisions of the business enterprise will not create future public opinions, demands, and policies that threaten the enterprise, its freedom, and its economic success."[21] Perhaps we need to aim at forming health care semicorporations—those with the priority of voluntary innovation over commercial marketing. Moreover, the cost efficiency of for-profit health care is open to debate. A recent *New England Journal of Medicine* editorial, citing the most up-to-date research, concludes: "Judged not as businesses but as hospitals which are supposed to serve the public interest, [for-profit hospitals] have been less cost-effective than their not-for-profit counterparts." The editorial was especially critical of the costs of corporate headquarters being allocated to individual hospitals and their communities.[22]

HMOs as a growth industry

Q: What earned $51.2 million in profits and produced a median return on equity of 29.5 percent—more than 2½ times the level of the Fortune 500?

A: What some consider a form of socialized medicine.[23]

One of the most fascinating recent developments is the selling of the social reform prepaid group practice movement as the HMO growth industry. This phenomenon has been reinforced by the Reagan administration, which has moved the government from an HMO venture capitalist role to one of promoting HMO investment by the private sector. In the fall of 1980, for example, the Department of Health and Human Services (HHS) announced a policy to encourage private investors to acquire federally-funded HMOs.[24] A year later it began a push for HMOs to convert to for-profit status.[25] Interestingly, investment can also support not-for-profit status. Group Health Cooperative of Puget Sound, the Seattle-based, not-for-profit HMO, has proven attractive to investors in the bond market.[26] Another HMO cooperative, Group Health Plan (St. Paul), has received a $5.4 million loan from the National Consumer Co-op Bank.[27]

Touche Ross, a consulting firm, has just prepared for HHS *The 1983 Investor's Guide to Health Maintenance Organizations.* This very useful study concludes that the HMO industry has reached a point of maturity—one worthy of investment. Moreover, the study demonstrates that HMOs are largely past the shaky start-up years and show high price-to-earnings ratios.[28] Enrollment has grown 11 percent per year since 1971.[29] Today's 275 HMOs have nearly 12 million people enrolled,[30] with market penetration highest in the West and upper Midwest.[31] All these factors have led to some recent investment activity,[32] perhaps the most interesting being the emergence of national HMO firms.[33]

Dr. Paul Ellwood, a strong advocate of national HMO corporations, cites Kaiser as the prime example. Upon closer inspection, however, it is clear that Kaiser operates as a set of semiautonomous regional operations. Moreover, some program leaders disagree with Ellwood. They believe that the national HMO concept is too monolithic and urge local diversity of sponsorship.[34] Indeed, Ellwood's long-time associate, Walter McClure, has compared HMO evolution to that of supermarkets.[35] Looking at the decline of the A&P in the face of stiff competition from excellent local and regional competitors, the implication of this analogy is that the potential of the national HMO firm approach may well be overstated, though several such corporations are emerging.

This focus on the bottom line is in keeping with the growing industrialization of the health care field. The question is whether this will lead to the HMO movement becoming dominated by the marketing concept. The Humana for-profit hospital chain has been rumored to be interested in HMO diversification.[36] This is a radical marketing concept-driven firm which emphasizes "customers," "feeders," and "profits." Humana is merchandising medical commodities as *Fortune* reports:

> Humana thinks of itself as serving not patients but "customers," and it woos them aggressively with newspaper ads, elaborate food, fast service and Holiday Inn-like private rooms with bath and color TV. (Chairman) Jones has given

up tactlessly comparing his hospitals to McDonald's hamburger franchises, but he still aims to offer a product standardized from California to Florida. . . . Humana advertises one-minute emergency care and sends out Insta-Care cards that play on people's fears of helplessness in a crisis.[37]

Here we can see Goldsmith's value concerns being left far behind. The future here is in a radical, narrow vision of the mass production and mass merchandising of service. The clearest articulator of this postindustrial world is Harvard's Theodore Levitt.

THE INDUSTRIALIZATION OF SERVICE

Some people contend that the production of personal services can and ought to be industrialized much as we have industrialized the production of goods. They see this happening in our postindustrial society. *Postindustrial society* refers to the shift of modern economies from the production of goods to the production of services. In this postindustrial context, the *HMO* term raises two questions: What is health maintenance? How shall it be produced?

Dr. Malcomb C. Todd, former president of the AMA, discussed the matter this way:

> The use of such terms as "health consumer" and "health provider" continue to foster the illusion that health is some kind of product which physicians can provide and patients consume. By definition, it is inferred that HMOs can effectively "maintain the health" of enrollees. The truth is that good health is a responsibility rather than a product, and that responsibility begins with the individual, with what each person does or does not do to maintain his or her own health.[38]

Dr. John Smillie, of the Kaiser-Permanente Medical Group program in Oakland writes:

> We agree with the concept of a competitive, pluralistic system when fee-for-service and prepaid group practice physicians practice in the same community. This system provides incentives for fee-for-service physicians to be more efficient and for prepaid group practice physicians to provide more personalized care.[39]

Here is the challenge that Elliot Richardson pointed out—to find a balance between humanistic personalism and industrial efficiency.

Theodore Levitt has made the prepaid group practice/postindustrial society connection most provocatively.[40] In the postindustrial society, he suggests, people gain more and more entitlements from government for basic rights and benefits while at the same time the economy becomes less productive as it shifts its concentration from goods to services.[41] Levitt believes that this dilemma can be resolved by applying management practices to the production of services—he calls this *the industrialization of service.* As strongly as

I argue that certain role innovators spearhead change, Levitt argues that today's industrialized, science-based society did not just happen, but was made to happen by a certain class of role innovators—namely, managers. Technology was not enough; someone had to organize, implement, and market these new modes of production. Henry Ford, for example, applied the idea of goods as the assembly of parts to the production of automobiles.[42]

Levitt suggests that management practices and technological applications be carried over into the production of services. He downgrades humanistic values. The nationwide chain of McDonald's hamburger outlets is his prime example of how productive this transfer can be. In his view, McDonald's Corporation has four customer-satisfying ingredients—rapid delivery at convenient locations; uniform, high quality of prepared foods; low prices; and a clean, orderly, and cheerful environment.[43] Two principles make this attractive hamburger delivery system efficient—the substitution of technology for people, and the capacity of this technology to control peoples' behavior. Levitt writes: "McDonald's restaurants are factories in the field—designed and equipped to do only what the planners intended, nothing more or less. Discretion is the enemy of order, standardization, and in this case, quality."[44]

On the customer side of this process, spontaneity is the enemy of satisfaction. Levitt approvingly describes how "the practice of McDonald's is to create an impression of abundance and generosity by slightly overfilling each bag of french fries,"[45] while at the same time using a specifically designed scoop to rigidly control the amount of fries put into each bag. By carefully designing all service aspects, 'satisfaction' is engineered into the experience of eating at McDonald's.

Levitt views this as a praiseworthy pioneering step in the industrialization of service. He asserts that service has lagged behind manufacturing in productivity because the former has thought "humanistically" while the latter has thought "technocratically and managerially" about its functions. Thus, Levitt disagrees with those health maintenance proponents who see the value of personal responsibility to be at the core of efforts to reform health care. Indeed, he cites the Kaiser prepaid group practice program as an example of technocratic thought applied to a basic personal service:

> But the industrialization of health care is not limited to diagnostics. During World War II, the Kaiser Foundation established the nation's first "health maintenance organization (HMO). . . ." There are now hundreds of such HMOs—mostly operated as profit-making firms. Large prepaid group membership rolls facilitate economies of scale and sound management, which in turn produce a full range of high-convenience, top-quality medical care at rock-bottom costs.[46]

This description is both wrong and one-dimensional. Most HMOs are not-for-profit, and very large HMOs are not automatically convenient. HMOs are good buys, not basement bargains. His description of prepaid group practice is one-sided in much the same way as was the HMO strategy—here the management principle is seen as *the* key to innovation success. Nonetheless, the insight about prepaid group practices being *somewhat* industrialized is valid. Let us see how far prepaid group practices can usefully be understood in the image of hamburger delivery systems. To do this, we need to look at concrete experience.

LIMITS TO INDUSTRIALIZATION

The lessons of Kaiser-Permanente

The excellent Kaiser-Permanente program has been the most successful example of a symbiotic medical-industrial relationship. Therefore, it offers some critical insights into the industrialization of service and its limits. A basic characteristic of industrialization is that quantity—institutional growth—becomes a basic imperative. In the early 1950s, Henry Kaiser imposed this imperative onto the Kaiser-Permanente medical program. He said, "I want to see a thousand of these health centers all over the country."[47] The program's physicians, however, feared that such marketplace growth in quantity would jeopardize the program's excellence. They feared that the lay board's unilateral business decisions were limiting professional discretion.

This tension had turned to outright disagreement by 1955, and the program was nearing a crisis point. A series of medical staff-management meetings were held at Lake Tahoe to find a way to resolve this conflict and to organizationally renew the mutuality of interest that had characterized the program. These meetings were successful. The "Tahoe Commitment" defined the program not in power-over terms of ownership and control, but in power-with terms of task and responsibility. It recognized that health care organization has three responsibilities—professional, business, and social.

> Accepting all this, no one can deny that patient care is the responsibility of physicians; nor can doctors deny that those trained in corporate management have something to add in the operation of medical systems. It is not simply administrative know-how. It is not merely a profit-making disposition. It is a willingness to take risks, and accept the financial responsibility inherent in such risks, in order to achieve well-defined but venturesome goals.[48]

This crisis, then, vividly clarifies the essential character of prepaid group practice organizational culture, revealing it as a system of shared responsibilities. One lesson here is that industrialization of service is appreciated by Kaiser physicians *up to a point,* after which they see it hampering rather than enhancing their professional practice; that is, industrialization (or the business task) has limits from the perspective of the program's professional task.

Three health responsibilities and three levels of prevention

Kerr L. White divides prevention into three categories which parallel Kaiser's three tasks. First, "containment, amelioration, or care of clinical disease" which has to do with "effective organization of care, appropriate staffing, and a sense of responsibility for the continued surveillance of patients who have been hospitalized or are at risk of being hospitalized."[49]

As part of this *professional* task, he suggests that visiting nurses be used for people recovering at home from cardiac failure episodes. Second, White suggests that *screening procedures,* technologized testing to detect disease early, can be used. He is skeptical, however, about this *industrial* approach to prevention since little is known about the natural history of various diseases. Third is "the primary prevention of disease" which has three elements— immunization procedures for high risk groups, environmental factors, and personal behavior. These elements roughly parallel a broad interpretation of the *social* task of a prepaid group practice program. White sees great potential in this area, but observes that it involves enormous shifts of basic cultural and social values.

Garfield's industrial model of health care

Since it began, the Kaiser-Permanente program has had preventive services as a basic principle.[50] Nonetheless, until recently, little programmatic emphasis had been put on such services as the state of the art and its cost in this aspect of health care over the years did not seem to justify too great an investment. Still, the program's subscriber policies listed preventive services as an assured service, and this raised two questions from the perspective of Kaiser-Permanente's *industrial task:* What would be the impact on medical resources if everyone acted on their entitlement to an annual checkup? What would be the cost? Here we see the issues of the postindustrial society as posed by Levitt—increasing entitlement and pressure for saving money by increasing productivity. Indeed, this is precisely the way that Dr. Garfield, the program's inventor, sees the basic issue of American health care generally.[51]

> The traditional medical care system has an input (the patient), a processing unit of discrete medical resources (individual doctors and individual hospitals) and an outcome (one hopes, the cured or improved patient). Customarily the patient decides when he needs care. This more or less educated decision by the patient creates a variable entry mix into medical care consisting of (1) the well, (2) the "worried well," (3) the "early sick," and (4) the sick.[52]

He goes on to note that in the traditional system, the fee (for each service) sometimes delays a person in seeking medical attention. The Kaiser prepayment mechanism eliminates this problem. However, the fee also acts as a "regulator of flow into the system." Thus, Kaiser prepayment, in Dr. Garfield's view, results in an "uncontrolled flood" of "worried well" people into the Kaiser system. He sees the same pattern happening in America in general as third-party prepayment expands. He proposes to use health testing—preventive services—as a new regulator to use resources more productively.[53]

Over the years, Kaiser has experimented with a pilot project that produces annual physicals on a mass production basis. These physicals are similar to the very comprehensive annual checkups given to corporate executives (largely as tokens of prestige, one suspects) in the scope of what is tested for, but dissimilar in that they are not done by physicians but by paraprofessionals and computerized technology. They are, then, a perfect example of the industrialization of health maintenance service. As envisioned by Garfield, this screening service would become the new point of entry into the medical care system by triaging (assessing and referring) people to appropriate resources. The "worried well," for example, would no longer flow directly to the physician, but would be directed to other specialists, such as health educators.

Thus, while the program, by its prepaid comprehensive set of benefits, would give the impression of an abundance of services, it would have a device in its screening service—like the McDonald's french fry scooper—to rigidly control utilization. It is important to note that the multiphasic screening techniques were developed to meet the increasing demand for annual checkups, and Garfield's suggested use of these techniques as a new system regulator is to meet the increasing demand for services generally.

Although it is Dr. Garfield's unique genius to view health care from the perspective of the industrial task—he is the closest person that the health care field has to a great organizational tinkerer like Henry Ford—he also has identified the relevance of industrialized health maintenance services to the professional and person-social tasks. He observes that by using screening as an entry point, the health care system can be made more orderly with clearer pathways for the patient to follow. This creates enormous opportunities to shift from episodic care to continuity of care. From the professional perspective, continuity of care would enable physicians to more responsibly use their skills on chronic conditions, which is now the dominant disease pattern. Further, Garfield sees health testing as creating new opportunities to give relevant, personalized instruction to people concerning identified problems and to promote health.[54]

Face-to-face relationships cannot be industrialized

David Mechanic, a medical sociologist, has criticized Garfield's industrial approach. Mechanic begins with Goldsmith's nonmarketing concept concerns—health care services are face-to-face relationships which involve the professional task, the physician-patient relationship, and continuity of care. First, Mechanic refutes Garfield's contention that fee-for-service is a major regulator of physician usage by citing Kaiser data showing that Kaiser members make the same number of physician visits per year as non-Kaiser members in the fee-for-service sector. Second, he notes that most people who seek primary care have self-limiting, contagious, acute illnesses for which multiphasic screening would be inappropriate.[55] Third, it is hard to sort out and categorize people whose medical symptoms and life stresses are closely connected. Fourth, the authority of the physician is often a crucial element in the care of such people, and a technological sorting process may harmfully separate the physician from the patient labeled "worried well."[56] Mechanic believes that the health care field needs new ways of preserving humanistic, personalized relationships with patients in the face of the increasing bureaucratization of medicine.

A role innovator approach to prevention

As we have seen, a basic issue in HMOs is the tension between efficiency and personalism. In the Garfield model, the issue is resolved strongly in favor of efficiency where a technological screening device regulates peoples' access to physicians. On the other hand, other new approaches emphasize the need for responsible people to regulate technological tools—they see the personal element as being central. David Mechanic makes the following suggestion as one way to counteract a tendency for organized systems of care to overstress efficiency at the expense of personalism:

> Models for the future must . . . develop entirely new type workers whose prime concerns will be the continuity of health care, the health education of the patient, and the coordination of the technical and social aspects of health care service. Such new elements must not be mechanisms to draw off patients who "waste" the physicians' time; they must be, rather, an integral part of the entire health service, bringing together what technical developments and increasing organization have segmented.[57]

He goes on to suggest a form of a "medical ombudsman" to be the organizational agent for making care more wholistic; that is, coordinated around the person's needs. This is, of course, a role-innovator approach to the problem.

Kaiser listens to the customer

Health care, then, includes three tasks or responsibilities—professional, industrial, and sociopersonal. Sociopersonal responsibility is not just a theoretical addition to Kaiser-Permanente's corporate definition. Rather, prepaid group practices, such as Kaiser and Group Health Cooperative, are beginning to seriously move in the direction of personal responsibility, health promotion, and self-care.[58] Kaiser has recently decided to streamline its "approach to population health screening emphasizing those areas in which there is reasonable expectation that early diagnosis will affect outcome and reinforce our efforts at patient education."[59] This is an example of the professional and sociopersonal tasks limiting the industrial task. Industrially organized screening is modified to better serve medical practice and personal responsibility.

Moreover, Kaiser, for all its excellence, is beginning to suffer in the marketplace by its "factory" image, and is experimenting to find ways to deliver its services in a more convenient and personal fashion. This has attracted some favorable attention. *Consumer Reports* has noted that some Kaiser subscribers are being assigned to medical groups that are organized to give more personalized service.[60] More recently, the *New York Times* called attention to Kaiser's building of satellite ambulatory health centers at locations more convenient to its membership.[61] Indeed, access to personalized health care services may, in the opinion of some HMO leaders, emerge as the key competitive edge. One HMO leader puts it this way:

> The 70s have made us conscious of cost containment. But, in the 80s I think we will have to be more responsive to our subscribers and potential subscribers in terms of their preconceived needs, in terms of paying more attention to questions of access . . . to amenities . . . to middle class values. . . . Some of that change will be due to the increase in available physicians and the increase in access to the fee-for-service system.[62]

THEORY V: PRINCIPLES OF VOLUNTARISM FOR SURVIVAL CURVE MANAGERS

An era of ideals, hard choices, and megatrends

Organizational cultures are dominated by ideals. Traditionally, health care's organizational culture has been dominated by, in Paul Starr's view, "The ideals of professionalism and voluntarism, which softened the underlying acquisitive activity. The restraint exercised by those ideals now grows weaker. The health center of one era is the profit center of the next."[63] While Jeff Goldsmith is more enthusiastic about the corporatization of health care, he shares Starr's concern about these traditional ideals. He writes:

> There is no reason why the modern health care enterprise cannot be managed humanely and why it cannot provide the framework for a satisfying practice. Health care managers must insist upon the maintenance of human values in the operation of their facilities.[64]

He expresses this as a challenge of entrepreneurship. I would say that it is a challenge of social entrepreneurship—one that involves agreement building and innovation. We have entered an era of conspicuous choice.

American health care has moved through a number of eras. Our present arrangements were first begun around the turn of the century in an era of conspicuous altruism as millionaires across the nation funded our unique, voluntary, not-for-profit community hospitals. After World War II came an era of conspicuous hospital construction backed by federal Hill-Burton funds, and with the 1950s came an era of conspicuous consumption as an increasing number of Americans began to receive health insurance as a tax-free fringe benefit at their place of employment. With exploding technology and aging populations, the Medicare-Medicaid years have been an era of conspicuous cost. With turbulent times, we must now make some basic choices. Starr believes that health care voluntarism has decomposed. He puts the issue in traditional either/or terms of public versus private sectors.

> The failure to rationalize medical services under public control meant that sooner or later they would be rationalized under private control. . . . Instead of public financing for prepaid plans that might be managed by the subscribers' chosen representatives, there will be corporate financing for private plans controlled by conglomerates whose interests will be determined by the rate of return on investments. That is the future toward which American medicine now seems to be headed. . . . Whether it does depends on choices that Americans have still to make.[65]

I want to suggest, however, that voluntarism—Theory V—can be renewed as an ideal that can shape our health care field. Starr's suggestion of a system of consumer-governed HMOs could be, I believe, a *voluntary*—not public—strategy. This can only happen, however, if we keep the dual nature of social enterprise in view. Recent overemphasis on impersonal bureaucratic-economic forces and technical-corporate fixes hides the hard political choices ahead. Robert B. Reich reminds us that by balancing the political and economic factors, we preserve both our individual autonomy and our sense of belonging to some larger, meaningful community. Moreover, he says that this balancing act will be done in our society by people making hard choices at the local level.[66]

Principles of health care voluntarism for turbulent times

Drawing on the ground covered in this book and widening our horizon by carefully bringing to bear Robert Sigmond's pathbreaking thoughts on health care voluntarism,[67] I want to conclude with some general principles for health care voluntarism in its turbulent present and future. Besides tapping the ideas of Schon, Follett, Drucker, Peters and Waterman, and others, I also want to use some terms from John Naisbitt's *Megatrends*. He has clarified and documented the social trends—the patterns of innovative choices—that are emerging as guiding ones for the last quarter of this century. His terms are useful additions to the survival curve manager's vocabulary for discussing successful health care institution building.

1. *People, not delivery systems, produce health.* Health is something that individuals generate, often in cooperation with family, friends, and community. Self- and mutual help are prime determinants of health. Naisbitt refers to this as the shift from institutional help to self-help.[68]

2. *Health service arrangements are the cooperative interaction of consumers, providers, and managers all working together within the wider network of friends, family, and community.* This reflects the shift from autocratic bureaucracies to cooperative networking.[69] Networking gives people a sense of belonging that is essential for efficiency. The voluntary sector is anchored in such networks.

3. Since disease, death, and so on, are generally not conquerable, and since our aging population is shifting its allegiance from physicians to costly medical technology itself, *the voluntary pursuit of affordability has to be tempered by the emergence of an involved, informed citizenry that can put technologized medicine in human and economic perspective.* This is the shift from forced technology (e.g., Levitt's industrialization of health) to high tech/ high touch (e.g., Mechanic's humane caregivers).[70]

4. *There will be increasing local citizen-consumer activism as a new social consensus concerning health care is formed.* Such a loyal constituency is essential to politically protect the health care field as it strives to maintain access to quality, affordable service. This is the trend from representative to participatory democracy.[71]

5. *Since health is basically a cooperative and local phenomenon, the independent, not-for-profit sector, which is the force that best operates cooperatively at the local level, should take the lead in developing new health care arrangements.* Moreover, since the voluntary sector was cowed in the previous placid period by regulatory and marketplace thrusts, and fought to defend the status quo, it may be useful to call leaders in today's turbulent environment *neovoluntarists.* These reformers are dedicated to cooperatively developing more disciplined, affordable, and competing health care arrangements. Naisbitt interprets this emphasis on tackling problems at the local level as part of the general shift from centralization to decentralization.[72] The methods will be debate, negotiation, and compromise.

6. *Health and health care services are too important to be left to any one of the three basic social forces—cooperation, regulation, and competition.* Over the last 20 years, competition and regulation have preoccupied our attention. Voluntarism eschews the "final victory" of any one force and seeks a proper balance of all three forces reflecting the realities, the laws, of our

situation. In competition it sees a method that can provide the consumer with affordable choices, in regulation it sees the means to assure that competition is fair, and in cooperation it sees a method to choose a social direction for institution building (as well as the means to initiate it and to develop a loyal citizenry to support it and hold it accountable). I would call this the trend from either/or to balanced policy.

7. *Health service arrangements are actually local health care political alliances.* In placid times, these arrangements were relatively stable. With the turbulence of the 1980s, these alliances have moved beyond a stable state. We have entered an era of coalition and institution building.

8. *Striving to escape from the model myopia of other reformers, voluntarists see a need for a plurality of arrangements.* These arrangements range from relatively unstructured ones stressing high-touch service through competitive generic health care arrangements, such as HMOs, to very structured ones emphasizing the hospital as an emporium of high technology. This variety will give both consumers and providers a diversity of choices. This is part of a general social shift from either/or to multiple options.[73]

9. *The voluntaristic concept of quality will be enlarged to include prudent management of resources.* With the shift in our disease patterns from acute to chronic conditions comes a need for well-articulated health care arrangements so that patients can be appropriately referred and followed in their treatment. Arrangements that squander resources with no discipline become disarticulated and thereby create barriers to proper, continuous care. Therefore, sound management that can provide such discipline becomes another dimension of quality.

10. *Affordability, then, is a pressure for rearranging American health care and a goal.* Making affordable health care a goal is more than a quantitative concern over aggregate health care costs. It is also a qualitative search for better articulated and directed arrangements. It also raises the broader question of how we will rank and relate health care with other often related social values, such as housing, education, transportation, national defense, and so on.

11. *Voluntarists believe that social learning and change happen best in a local, retail fashion.* They do not believe in wholesale change by government or corporate fiat. As pluralists they do not seek panacea-type solutions, but are pledged to relentless, undramatic gradualism in bettering our social arrangements. In this view, the everyday, real drama is in working better with one another. In short, voluntarism in turbulent times favors widespread, steady, coordinated incremental institution building. *Organizational cultures will be renewed by creating exemplary innovations such as HMOs.*

12. *Catalytic community leadership is decisive.* Renegotiating our local health care alliances requires community health political leadership. Leader-

ship by manager, provider and consumer innovation patrons, champions, and young Turks needs to be concerned with improving the performance of particular health care arrangements by means of improving consumer, provider, and manager cooperation—the pursuit of common purposes disciplined by an enlarged sense of duty and citizenship. Leadership will be catalytic rather than charismatic.

13.   As the voluntaristic trends towards high touch, affordability, consumerism, and so on become obvious, *traditional professional ideals* and incentives (such as peer approval, pride of caring craftsmanship, maintenance of excellent standards, avoidance of ridicule, and altruism) *will grow stronger.*

14.   *Voluntarism's goal goes beyond survival to success.* Voluntarism strives to build and preserve value-driven institutions impelled towards excellence.

15.   *In turbulent times, hospitals and other health care institutions can survive and succeed by selectively cooperating to pursue competitive advantage. This involves a stress on entrepreneurial innovation for excellence by means of negotiated agreements, especially between providers and insurers.*

16.   *In thinking about what business they are in, hospitals must seek to excel in sick care organizational innovation while reinforcing—not replacing or eroding—natural personal, family, and community caring networks.* This is the trend from short- to long-term view.[74]

17.   *Excellent health care institutions must be concerned with their community's success.* By contributing to social cohesion, excellent health care institutions reduce social incoherence and advance democracy. *They not only create customers, they also care for patients, encourage citizen participation, and earn loyalty.* This reflects their triple purpose—entrepreneurial, professional, and social. Hospitals will survive if their managers pursue community success. Survival curve managers must do what is civically necessary. This is what I call the *trend of civic necessity.* As Emily Friedman has noted, survival curve managers must not carry the marketing concept too far; they must not become too narrow in their customer population. She offers the positive example of a hospital which is surviving in New York City where 25 percent of the hospital beds have been eliminated. She reports that its administrator has said: "Our plan is to do what the people *need* us to do, not what we *want* to do."[75] She goes on to observe: "As a result . . . his hospital does not offer certain kinds of tertiary care, but it does offer classes in English as a second language and volunteer school crossing guards."[76] Follett's Law of the Situation not only points to the marketing concept, but also points to the social culture that envelops the marketplace. Many hospitals that succeed as community integrators will survive. Health care politics is not only the art of the marketplace possible, but also the art of the socially necessary. Ultimately, the health care survival curve leads toward community excellence.

Finally, health care entrepreneurship in the turbulent 1980s will be difficult with role innovators constantly tempted to do the expedient thing. Perhaps the key is what the Romans called *gravitas*. As Eric Sevareid has suggested:

> What counts most in the long haul of adult life is not the brilliance or charisma or derring-do, but rather the quality that the Romans call "gravitas"—patience, stamina, and weight of judgment . . . The prime virtue is courage because it makes the other virtues possible.[77]

Social entrepreneurship's challenge, then, is to manage the health care survival curve, and to balance competition and cooperation guided by *gravitas* so that institutions succeed and communities are well served.

NOTES

Chapter 6

1. Jeff C. Goldsmith, *Can Hospitals Survive?* (Homewood, Ill.: Dow Jones-Irwin, 1981), p. 2.

2. Ibid. Quotation from Peter F. Drucker, *The Practice of Management* (New York: Harper & Row, 1954), p. 37.

3. Goldsmith, *Can Hospitals Survive?* p. 2.

4. Ibid., p. 3.

5. John Naisbitt, *Megatrends* (New York: Warner Books, 1982), p. 85.

6. Theodore Levitt, "Management and the Post-Industrial Society," *The Public Interest* 44 (Summer 1976), pp. 69–103. See also T. Levitt, "The Industrialization of Service," *Harvard Business Review,* September-October 1976, pp. 63–74.

7. Goldsmith, *Can Hospitals Survive?* p. 102.

8. Ibid., p. 140.

9. Ibid., p. 203.

10. Ibid., p. 204.

11. Ibid., p. 5.

12. Ibid., p. 102.

13. Drucker, *The Practice of Management,* p. 39.

14. Ibid., pp. 37–39.

15. Thomas J. Peters and Robert H. Waterman, Jr., *In Search of Excellence* (New York: Harper & Row, 1982), pp. 12 and 85.

16. Remarks in *The Challenge of the Next Ten Years for HMOs,* ed. Avis Berman (Claverack, N.Y.: The Esselstyn Foundation, 1980), pp. 90–91.

17. Eric J. Cassell, M.D., "Our Sickness Care System," *The Wall Street Journal,* March 3, 1980, p. 16.

18. Drucker, *The Practice,* p. 389.

19. Ibid.

20. "The Upheaval in Health Care," *Business Week,* July 25, 1983, p. 56.

21. Drucker, *The Practice,* p. 385.

22. Arnold S. Relman, M.D., "Investor-owned Hospitals and Health Care Costs," *New England Journal of Medicine* 309, no. 6 (August 11, 1983), p. 372.

23. *Chicago Tribune* Business Section, June 7, 1983, p. 1.

24. "U.S. to Help Firms Acquire HMOs," *AMA News,* October 30, 1981, p. 1.

25. "Federal Government Touts HMO Movement," *AMA News,* November 6, 1981, pp. 1 and 11.

26. "Investors Eying HMOs," *Business Week,* June 14, 1982, p. 114.

27. *Group Health News,* December 1981, p. 7.

28. *The 1983 Investors' Guide to Health Maintenance Organizations* (Rockville, Md.: Department of Health and Human Services Publication, no. PHS 83-50202, 1983), p. 2.

29. Ibid., p. 3.

30. Ibid., p. 5.

31. Ibid., p. 6.

32. Ibid., p. 7–10.

33. Ibid., p. 13.

34. Berman, *The Challenge,* p. 10.

35. Ibid., p. 66.

36. Deborah H. Harrison and John R. Kimberly, "Private and Public Initiative in Health Maintenance Organizations," *Journal of Health Politics, Policy and Law* 7, no. 1 (Spring 1982), p. 83.

37. Gwen Kinkead, "Humana's Hard-Sell Hospitals," *Fortune,* November 17, 1980, pp. 68 and 76.

38. Malcolm C. Todd, M.D., "The AMA's View of HMOs," in *Proceedings of the 1975 Group Health Institute* (Washington, D.C.: Group Health Association of America, 1975), p. 20.

39. John Smillie, M.D., Letter to the Editor, "Operation of Kaiser-Permanente Program," *New England Journal of Medicine* 297, no. 1, p. 63.

40. See generally, Levitt, "Post-industrial Society," pp. 69–103.

41. Ibid., pp. 70–71.

42. Ibid., p. 74.

43. Ibid., p. 86.

44. Ibid., pp. 86–87.

45. Ibid., p. 92.

46. Ibid., p. 94.

47. Greer Williams, "Kaiser," *Modern Hospital,* February 1971, p. 70.

48. Ibid., p. 71.

49. See generally, Kerr L. White, "Prevention as a National Health Goal," *Preventive Medicine* 4, no. 3 (1975), pp. 247–51.

50. Williams, "Kaiser," p. 76.

51. Sidney R. Garfield, M.D., "The Delivery of Medical Care," *Scientific American* 222, no. 4 (April 1970), p. 15. Note: Dr. Garfield's views are his own and not Kaiser-Permanente policy. As we will see, the program has sponsored a long-term pilot based on his views to test them.

52. Ibid., p. 19.

53. Ibid., p. 20.

54. Sidney Garfield, M.D., "A Look at the Economics of Medical Care," in *Technology and Health Care Systems in the 1980s,* ed. Morris F. Collen, M.D. (Rockville, Md.: Department of Health, Education and Welfare, 1974), p. 175.

55. David Mechanic, "Human Problems and the Organization of Health Care," *The Annals of the American Academy of Political and Social Science,* January 1972, pp. 7–8.

56. Ibid., pp. 8–10.

57. Mechanic, "Human Problems," p. 10.

58. Anne Somers, "The Lifetime Health Monitoring Program," in *Proceedings of the 27th Annual Group Health Institute* (Washington, D.C.: Group Health Association of America), p. 302.

59. Jeffrey F. Fessell, M.D., Chief, Department of Medicine. The Permanente Medical Group, San Francisco Letter to the author (March 1981).

60. "The HMO Approach to Health Care," *Consumer Reports,* May 1982, p. 247.

61. N. R. Kleinfield, "The King of HMOs," *New York Times,* July 31, 1983, Section 3., p. 23.

62. Berman, *The Challenge,* p. 83.

63. Paul Starr, *The Social Transformation of American Medicine* (New York: Basic Books, 1982), p. 448.

64. Goldsmith, *Can Hospitals Survive?* p. 204.

65. Starr, *The Social Transformation,* p. 449.

66. Robert B. Reich, "Beyond Reaganomics," *The New Republic,* November 18, 1981, p. 25.

67. Robert M. Sigmond, "Quest for Excellence in Health Care: Balancing Cooperation, Competition and Regulation," presented at the Eighth Annual Health Forum of Northeast Ohio, Cleveland, 1980. Also see "Why Neither Competition

nor Regulation is the Whole Answer," *Trustee,* May 1980, pp. 35–38. Sigmond's work on redefining voluntarism has helped me enormously.

68. Naisbitt, *Megatrends,* pp. 131–142.

69. Ibid., pp. 192–96.

70. Ibid., pp. 39–40.

71. Ibid., p. 159.

72. Ibid., p. 129.

73. Ibid., p. 232.

74. Ibid., pp. 84–85.

75. Emily Friedman, "When the Mainstream Becomes a Trickle," *Hospital Forum,* July–August 1983, p. 17.

76. Ibid.

77. Quoted in James O. Hepner and Donna M. Hepner, *The Health Strategy Game* (St. Louis: C. V. Mosby, 1973), p. 248.

■ Bibliography

Aiken, Michael, and Robert R. Alford. "Community Action." *American Sociological Review,* August 1970, pp. 650–65.

Alinsky, Saul D. *John L. Lewis.* New York: Vintage Books, 1970.

Allison, Graham T. *Essence of Decision.* Boston: Little, Brown, 1971.

Anderson, Odin W. "All Health Care Systems Struggle Against Rising Costs." *Hospitals* 50 (October 1, 1976), pp. 97–103.

_____. *Blue Cross Since 1929* (Cambridge, Mass: Ballinger, 1975).

_____. "Foreword." In Jeff C. Goldsmith, *Can Hospitals Survive?* Homewood, Ill.: Dow Jones-Irwin, 1981.

"Are There a New Set of HMO Sponsors in the Wings?" *Group Health News,* March 1983, p. 2.

Bailey, F. G., ed. *Debate and Compromise: The Politics of Innovation.* Oxford: Basil Blackwell, 1973.

Bennis, Warren. *The Unconscious Conspiracy.* New York: Amacom, 1976.

Berman, Avis, ed. *The Challenge of the Next Ten Years for HMOs.* Claverack, N.Y.: The Esselstyn Foundation, 1980.

Bolan, Richard S. "Community Decision Behavior: The Culture of Planning." *AIP Journal,* September 1969, pp. 301–9.

Brown, Lawrence D. *Politics and Health Care Organization.* Washington, D.C.: The Brookings Institution, 1983.

Burns, Linda. "Lessons Learned through Hospital Involvement in HMOs." *Hospitals,* August 16, 1979, pp. 73–77.

Bylinsky, Gene. "Can Bell Labs Keep It Up?" *Fortune,* June 27, 1983, pp. 90–91.

Califano, Joseph. Remarks at HHS sponsored conference on HMOs. Washington, D.C., March 10, 1978.

Campbell, James C., M.D. "Hospitals and Physicians." In *Proceedings of the Twenty-Third Annual George Bugbee Symposium.* Chicago: Center for Health Administration Studies, June 1981, pp. 83–92.

Cassell, Eric J., M.D. "Our Sickness Care System," *The Wall Street Journal,* March 3, 1980, p. 16.

Champion, Hale. "Keynote Address." Presented at the 27th Annual Group Health Institute, Los Angeles, June 1977.

Chicago Tribune, June 7, 1983, Business Section.

Chu, Phillip, M.D. "Remarks on Alternative Delivery Systems." Delivered at Blue Cross Association meeting on Alternative Forms of Health Care Finance and Delivery, Kansas City, June 1970.

Commager, Henry S., ed. *Selections from the Federalists.* New York: Appleton-Century-Crofts, 1949.

Committee on the Costs of Medicare Care. *Medical Care for the American People.* Chicago: University of Chicago Press, 1932.

Community Programs for Affordable Health Care. Untitled brochure. Chicago: AHA, March 1982.

Connors, Edward J. "Multihospital Systems in the Changing Health Care Landscape." *Trustee,* July 1979, pp. 24–30.

Cutting, Cecil, M.D. "Historical Development and Operating Principles." In *The Kaiser-Permanente Medical Care Program,* ed. Anne Somers. New York: The Commonwealth Fund, 1971, pp. 17–22.

————. "Reflections of a Medical Director." Oakland, Calif.: Kaiser-Permanente Advisory Service, October 1976.

Davis, Aubrey. "Interaction of Board with Medical Staff and Administration." Presented at the Prepaid Group Practice School, Seattle, Washington, February 1972.

Davis, Milton S., and Robert E. Tranquada. "A Sociological Evaluation of the Watts Neighborhood Health Center." *Medical Care* 7, no. 2 (March–April 1969), pp. 105–17.

Deering, W. Palmer, and Irwin Miller. *The Role of Physician Leadership.* Chicago: BCA, 1975.

DeKruif, Paul. *Kaiser Wakes the Doctors.* New York: Harcourt Brace Jovanovich, 1943.

Dole, Charles E. "Mr. Auto Surveys Chrysler's Survival Course," *Christian Science Monitor,* April 21, 1983, p. 14.

Drucker, Peter F. *Managing In Turbulent Times.* London: Pan Books, paperback, 1981.

————. *Men, Ideas and Politics.* New York: Harper & Row, 1971.

Elinson, Jack, and Conrad Herr. "A Sociomedical View of Neighborhood Health Centers." *Medical Care* 8, no. 2 (March–April 1970), pp. 97–103.

Emery, F. E. and E. L. Trist. "The Causal Texture of Organizational Environments." *Human Relations* 18, 1965, pp. 21–32.

Falkson, Joseph L. *HMOs and the Politics of Health System Reform.* Chicago: American Hospital Association, 1980.

————. *An Evaluation of Alternative Models of Citizen Participation in Urban Bureaucracy.* Ann Arbor: Programs in Health Planning, School of Public Health, University of Michigan, 1971.

"Federal Government Touts HMO Movement." *AMA News,* November 6, 1981, pp. 1 and 11.

Fessell, Jeffrey F., M.D., Chief, Department of Medicine, The Permanente Medical Group, San Francisco (March 1981). Letter to the author.

Fisher, Robert, and William Ury. *Getting to Yes.* New York: Penguin Books, 1983.

Follett, Mary Parker. *The New State.* New York: Peter Smith, 1965 republication.

Friedman, Emily. "When the Mainstream Becomes a Trickle." *Hospital Forum,* July/August, 1983, pp. 9–17.

Fry, Ronald E. Book review of *Managing Change and Collaboration in the Health System.* In *NEJM* 303, no. 19 (November 6, 1980), pp. 1131–32.

Garfield, Sidney, M.D. "A Look at the Economics of Medical Care." In *Technology and Health Care Systems in the 1980's,* ed. Morris F. Collen, M.D. Rockville, Md.: DHEW, 1974, pp. 169–75.

Garfield, Sidney R., M.D. "The Delivery of Medical Care," *Scientific American* 222, no. 4 (April 1970), pp. 15–23.

"General Motors Will Sing out, Loud and Clear," *Perspective,* Summer 1976.

"Genesee Valley Group Health Association." In *The Complex Puzzle of Health Care Costs.* Washington, D.C.: President's Council on Wage & Price Stability, 1976, pp. 137–46.

Goldsmith, Jeff C. *Can Hospitals Survive?* Homewood, Ill.: Dow Jones-Irwin, 1981.

Gordon, Jeoffrey B. "The Politics of Community Medicine Projects: A Conflict Analysis. *Medical Care* 7, no. 6 November–December 1969, pp. 418–28.

Greenberg, Ira, and Michael Rodburg. "The Role of Prepaid Group Practice in Relieving the Medical Care Crisis." *Harvard Law Review* 84, no. 4 (February 1971).

Griffith, John R. "The Role of Blue Cross and Blue Shield in the Future U.S. Health System." *Inquiry,* Spring 1983, pp. 12–19.

Handschin, Richard, M.D. "Operating Principles of Group Health Cooperative of Puget Sound." Presented at the Prepaid Group Practice School, Seattle, Washington, February 1972).

Harrelson, E. Frank, and Kirk M. Donovan. "Consumer Responsibility in a Prepaid Group Practice Health Plan." *American Journal of Public Health* 65, no. 10 (October 1975), pp. 1077–86.

Harrison, Deborah H., and John R. Kimberly. "Private and Public Initiative in Health Maintenance Organizations." *Journal of Health Politics, Policy and Law* 7, no. 1 (Spring 1982), pp. 80–95.

Hepner, James O., and Donna M. Hepner. *The Health Strategy Game.* St. Louis: C. V. Mosby, 1973.

Herbert, Robert F., and Albert N. Link. *The Entrepreneur.* New York: Praeger Publishers, 1983.

Heyssel, Robert M., M.D., and Henry M. Seidel, M.D. "The Johns Hopkins Experience in Columbia, Maryland." *New England Journal of Medicine* 295, no. 22 (November 25, 1976), pp. 1225–31.

Hirschman, Albert O. *The Strategy of Economic Development.* New Haven: Yale University Press, 1958.

"HMO Approach to Health Care." *Consumer Reports,* May 1982, pp. 246–51.

"HMO Network in Des Moines Set for Summer." *Group Health News,* March 1983, p. 15.

Hochbaum, G. M. "Consumer Participation in Health Planning: Toward Conceptual Clarification." *American Journal of Public Health* 59, no. 9 (September 1969), pp. 1698–1705.

"Hospital Administrators Seek Medical Staff Cooperation." *AMA News,* March 18, 1983, p. 1.

Hurst, Ronald A. "What Does Management Think Should be Done About Containing Health Care Costs." In *Health Care in the American Economy: Number 3,* ed. David H. Klein and John F. Newman. Chicago: Blue Cross and Blue Shield Associations, 1980, pp. 51–56.

Inglehart, John K. "Health Care and American Business." *New England Journal of Medicine* 306, no. 2, (January 14, 1982), pp. 120–24.

Ingwerson, Marshall. "Cooperation Grows between Developers, Neighborhood groups." *Christian Science Monitor,* May 17, 1983, p. 4.

"Investors Eying HMOs." *Business Week,* June 14, 1982, p. 114.

Janowitz, Morris. *Social Control of the Welfare State.* New York: Elsevier, 1976.

Johnson, Everett A., and Richard L. Johnson. *Hospitals in Transition.* Rockville, Md.: Aspen Publication, 1982.

Kanter, Rosabeth Moss. "The Middle-Manager as Innovator." *Harvard Business Review,* July–August 1982, pp. 95–105.

Jarvis, Jean M. "The Innovators: Keys to Successful Organizational and Professional Entrepreneurship." *Hospital Forum,* July/August 1983, p. 38.

Kay, Raymond, M.D. *Historical Review of the Southern California Permante Medical Group.* Los Angeles: Southern California Permanente Medical Group, 1979.

Kinkead, Gwen. "Humana's Hard-Sell Hospitals." *Fortune,* November 17, 1980, pp. 68–83.

Kleinfield, N. R. "The King of HMOs," *The New York Times,* July 31, 1983, p. 23.

Kuhn, Thomas. *The Structure of Scientific Revolutions.* 2d ed. Chicago: University of Chicago Press, 1970.

Levitt, Theodore. "Management and the Post-Industrial Society." *Public Interest,* no. 44 (Summer 1976), pp. 69–103.

————. "The Industrialization of Service. *Harvard Business Review,* September–October 1976, pp. 63–74.

Light, H. L., and R. K. Match. "The Potential of the Teaching Hospital for the Development of Prepaid Group Practices." *Medical Care* 14, no. 8 (August 1976), pp. 643–53.

Lilley, William. Preface. In *The Complex Puzzle of Rising Health Care Costs.* Washington, D.C.: Council on Wage and Price Stability, December 1976.

"Lines Getting Blurred between M.D.'s, Hospitals." *AMA News,* June 24, 1983, p. 14.

Lipsky, Michael, and Morris Lounds. "Citizen Participation and Health Care: Problems of Government Induced Participation." *Journal of Health Politics, Policy and Law,* Spring 1976, pp. 85–111.

MacColl, William A. *Group Practice & Prepayment of Medical Care.* Washington, D.C.: Public Affairs Press, 1966.

Maddox, George, M.D., and Eugene Stead, M.D. "The Professional and Citizen Participation." In *Proceedings of the 1973 Duke University Hospital Forum.* Durham, N.C.: Duke University, 1973, pp. 66–76.

Malcolm, Jan, and Paul M. Ellwood, Jr., M.D. "Competitive Approach May Ease Problems in Delivery System." *Hospitals,* August 16, 1979, pp. 66–69.

"Marketing." In *Proceedings: 24th Annual Group Health Institute.* Washington, D.C.: GHAA, 1974.

Match, Robert, M.D. "The Keystone of the HMO: Its Medical Director." Presented at a Conference on the Medical Director in Prepaid Group Practice HMOs, Denver, April 1973.

McNerney, Walter J. "Containing Health Care Costs." In *Health Care in the American Economy: Number 3,* ed. David H. Klein and John F. Newman. Chicago: Blue Cross and Blue Shield Associations, 1980, pp. 61–67.

————. "Control of Health Care Costs In the 1980s. *The New England Journal of Medicine* 303, no. 19 (November 6, 1980), pp. 1088–95.

————. "Five Major Health Field Issues." *Hospital Financial Management* 30 (September 1976), p. 50.

————. "Health Care Coalitions." Paper presented at the 1982 Michael M. Davis Lecture, Center for Health Administration Studies, Chicago, May 1982.

————. "The Role of the Executive." *Hospital and Health Services Administration,* Fall 1976.

Mechanic, David. "Human Problems and the Organization of Health Care." *The Annals of the American Academy,* January 1972.

Mercer, Lyle. "The Role of The Member in Group Health Cooperative of Puget Sound." Presented at the HMOS Feedback Session, El Paso, Texas, December 1972.

Metcalf, Henry C., and L. Urwich, eds. *Dynamic Administration: Collected Papers of Mary Parker Follett.* New York: Harper & Row, 1940.

Meyer, Elizabeth M. "Renewed Voluntary Spirit Needed, Says Blue Cross." *Modern Health Care,* April 1977, pp. 55–56.

Moffat, Samuel. "Kaiser-Permanente: Prepaid Comes of Age." In *1977 Medical and Health Annual.* Chicago: Encyclopedia Britannica, 1977.

Mouat, Lucian. "Nader Tries to Get Air Travelers Consumer Group off the Ground." *Christian Science Monitor,* August 6, 1982, p. 6.

Morton, J. A. *Organizing for Innovation.* New York: McGraw-Hill, 1971.

Naisbitt, John. *Megatrends.* New York: Warner Books, 1982.

Neustadt, Richard E., and Harvey V. Fineberg, M.D. *The Swine Flu Affair.* Atlanta: Centers for Disease Control, HEW, 1978.

Nick, Ronald M. "Cooperative Planning—The Alternative Delivery System Coordinator Point of View." Paper presented at the Blue Cross Association Conference on Alternative Delivery System Planning, New Orleans, January 1975.

O'Donovan, Thomas R. "The Primary Care Initiative." *The Journal of Ambulatory Care Management,* February 1981, pp. 29–42.

Osmond, Humphrey, M.D. *Understanding Understanding.* New York: Bantam Books, 1974.

Ottensmeyer, David O., M.D. "Lessons from an HMO Launching." *Group Practice,* October 1973, pp. 29–31.

Perrott, George. *Federal Employee Health Benefits Programs: Utilization of Services.* Rockville, Md.: DHEW 1971.

Peters, Thomas J., and Robert H. Waterman, Jr. *In Search of Excellence.* New York: Harper & Row, 1982.

"Physicians' Roles in Corporations Debated." *AMA News,* March 18, 1983, pp. 6–7.

Pollack, Jerome. "The Union Health Movement as Voluntarism." *Voluntary Action and the State,* ed. Iago Goldston, M.D. New York: International Universities Press, 1961, pp. 105–21.

Porter, Michael E. "How Competitive Forces Shape Strategy." *Harvard Business Review,* March–April 1979, pp. 137–45.

"Private Sector Investment in Health Maintenance Organizations: A Case Study of Hospital Sponsorship." Rockville, Md.: DHHS Publication No. PHS 82-50183, June 1982.

Rafkind, Faith B. *Hospital Competitive Adaptation Strategy.* Masters thesis, Sloan School of Management, MIT, 1982.

Ready, R. K., and F. E. Ranelli. "Strategic and Nonstrategic Planning in Hospitals," *Health Care Management Review,* Fall 1982, pp. 27–38.

Reich, Robert B. "Beyond Reaganomics." *The New Republic,* November 18, 1981, pp. 19–25.

Reid, William. "Interorganizational Cooperation: A Review and Critique of Current Theory." In *Proceedings of Inter-Organizational Research in Health Conference,* ed. Paul E. White. HEW document PB 198 807. Springfield, Va.. National Technical Information Service, 1970.

Reinhold, Robert. "Competition Held Key to Lower Medical Cost." *The New York Times,* April 1, 1982, pp. 1 and 12.

Relman, Arnold S., M.D. "Investor-Owned Hospitals and Health Care Costs." *New England Journal of Medicine* 309, no. 6 (August 11, 1983), pp. 370–72.

Richardson, Elliot. *The Creative Balance.* New York: Holt, Rinehart & Winston, 1976.

Richardson, Elliot L. "Perspectives on the Health Revolution." *New England Journal of Medicine* 291, no. 6 (August 8, 1974), pp. 283–87.

Richman, Louis S. "Health Benefits Come under the Knife." *Fortune,* May 2, 1983, pp. 95–110.

Roberts, James, M.D., and Ernest Saward, M.D. "Letter to the Editor." *New England Journal of Medicine* 296, no. 10 (March 10, 1977), p. 578.

Rosen, George, M.D. "History and Health Care." *American Journal of Public Health* 67, no. 4 (April 1977), pp. 326–28.

Rosenberg, Conrad, M.D. "Physician Responsibility and Cooperative Planning." Delivered at BCA Conference on HMO Planning, New Orleans, 1975.

Saltman, Richard B., and David W. Young. "The Hospital Power Equilibrium. *Journal of Health Politics, Policy and Law* 6, no. 3. (Fall 1981), pp. 391–417.

Saward, Ernest S., M.D. "The Role of the Medical Director in the Group Practice HMO." Presented at a Conference on The Medical Director in Prepaid Group Practice Health Maintenance Organizations, Denver, April 1973.

Schon, Donald A. "Champions for Radical Innovation." *Harvard Business Review,* Fall 1973, pp. 77–86.

Schon, Donald A. *Technology and Change.* New York: Delacorte Press, 1967.

Shadid, Michael, M.D. *A Doctor for the People.* New York: Vanguard Press, 1939.

Sheldon, Alan. *Managing Change and Collaboration in the Health System.* Cambridge, Mass.: Oelgeschlager, Gunn and Hain, 1979.

Sigmond, Robert. "Why Neither Competition Nor Regulation is the Whole Answer." *Trustee,* May 1980, pp, 35–38.

Sigmond, Robert M. "Quest for Excellence in Health Care: Balancing Cooperation, Competition and Regulation." Presented at the Eighth Annual Health Forum of Northeast Ohio, Cleveland, June 1980.

Smillie, John, M.D. "Operation of Kaiser-Permanente Program," Letter To The Editor, *New England Journal of Medicine* 297, no. 1 (July 7, 1977), p. 62.

Somers, Anne. "The Lifetime Health Monitoring Program." In *Proceedings of the 27th· Annual Group Health Institute.* (Washington, D.C.: GHAA, 1977), pp. 285–302.

Somers, Anne E., ed. *The Kaiser-Permanente Medical Care Program.* New York: The Commonwealth Fund, 1971.

Starr, Paul. "Changing the Balance of Power in American Medicine." *Milbank Memorial Fund Quarterly* 58, no. 1 (1980), pp. 167–71.

_____. *The Social Transformation of American Medicine.* New York: Basic Books, 1982.

_____. "The Undelivered Health System." *The Public Interest,* no. 42 (Winter 1976), pp. 66–85.

Steiner, Jesse Frederick. "The Social Unit Experiment." In *Community Organization in Action,* ed. E. Harper and A. Durham. New York: Association Press, 1959, pp. 121–26.

Steinhauer, Bruce, M.D. "HMO Impact on Hospitals: The Possibilities and Realities." In *Prepaid Health Plans.* Chicago: Chicago Hospital Council, 1983, pp. 19–29.

Stevens, William K. "High Medical Costs Under Attack: A Drain on the Nation's Economy." *The New York Times,* March 28, 1982, pp. 1 and 18.

Stoeckle, John D., and Candib, Lucy M. "The Neighborhood Health Center—Reform

Ideas of Yesterday and Today." *The New England Journal of Medicine* 280, no. 25 (June 19, 1968), pp. 1385–90.

Stewart, Dave. "The HMO Challenge." Presented at the BCA HMO Marketing Conference, Dallas, March 1976.

Swanson, Steven. "Sale of Health Group Poses People versus Profits Issue." *Chicago Tribune,* April 23, 1981, pp. 1–2.

The 1983 Investors' Guide to Health Maintenance Organizations. Rockville, Md.: DHHS Publication, No. PHS 83-50202, 1983.

"The Malady of Health Care." *NOVA* television series. Boston: WGBN, 1981.

"The Upheaval in Health Care." *Business Week* July 25, 1983, p. 56.

Thompson, James D. "Thoughts on Inter-Organizational Relations." In *Inter-Organizational Research in Health: Conference Proceedings,* ed. Paul E. White. Rockville, Md.: DHEW, 1971, pp. 156–67.

"U.S. to Help Firms Acquire HMOs." *AMA News,* October 30, 1981, p. 1.

van Steenwyk, John. "The Insurer Role in HMO Planning and Development." Paper presented at the Blue Cross Association Conference on Alternative Delivery System Planning, New Orleans, January 1975.

Warden, Gail, and Edward Tuller. "HMOs and Hospitals: What Are the Options." *Hospitals,* August 16, 1979, pp. 63–65.

Weal, Betsy. "Northcare: HMO with Promise." *Modern Health Care,* June, 1975, pp. 61–65.

Weinerman, E. Richard, M.D. "Patients' Perceptions of Group Medicine Care." *American Journal of Public Health* 54, no. 6 (June 1964), pp. 880–89.

Weisbord, Marvin R. "Why Organization Development Hasn't Worked (so far) in Medical Centers." *Health Care Management Review,* Spring 1976, pp. 17–28.

White, Kerr L. "Prevention as a National Health Goal." *Preventive Medicine* 4, no. 3 (1975), pp. 247–51.

White, Paul, ed. *Inter-Organizational Research In Health: Conference Proceedings.* Rockville, Md.: DHEW, 1971.

"Will Hospitals Close?" *AMA News,* June 24, 1983, pp. 3 and 19.

Williams, Greer. "Kaiser." *Modern Hospital,* February 1971, pp. 67–95.

Yedidia, Avram. *Planning and Implementation of the Community Health Foundation.* Washington, D.C.: PHS-HEW, 1969.

Young, Paul. "HMO Cooperative Planning." Presented at the BCA Conference on Alternative Delivery System Planning. New Orleans: January 21, 1975.

————. Letter to the author, January 25, 1976.

————. Remarks at the Blue Cross Association Annual Board Meeting, Chicago, May 1974.

————. "Special Report: Prepaid Group Practice." Cincinnati: Blue Cross, 1972.

Zink, Victor. "As Others See Us." *Hospitals,* March 6, 1976, pp. 65–67.

Index